CYCLIC TABLES
OF
HINDU AND MAHOMEDAN CHRONOLOGY
REGARDING THE HISTORY
OF
THE TELUGU AND KANNADI
COUNTRIES

CYCLIC TABLES
OF
HINDU AND MAHOMEDAN CHRONOLOGY
REGARDING THE HISTORY
OF
THE TELUGU AND KANNADI
COUNTRIES

TO WHICH ARE ADDED THE

GENEALOGIES OF PARTICULAR HINDU FAMILIES,
WITH ESSAYS ON VARIOUS MATTERS OF ENQUIRY

CHARLES PHILIP BROWN

GYAN

Published by

GYAN

Gyan Publishing House
5, Ansari Road
Daryaganj, New Delhi-110002
Phone: 011-47034999, 9811692060
E-mail: books@gyanbooks.com

Distribution Network
gyanbooks.com
India, USA, Canada, UK, Australia, France

ISBN : 978-81-212-3289-0 (PB)
First Published, 1850

2nd Impression 2020

Printed at: Gyan Press, Delhi.

CYCLIC TABLES

OF

HINDU AND MAHOMEDAN

CHRONOLOGY,

REGARDING THE HISTORY OF

THE TELUGU AND KANNADI COUNTRIES

TO WHICH ARE ADDED THE

GENEALOGIES OF PARTICULAR HINDU FAMILIES, WITH ESSAYS ON VARIOUS MATTERS OF ENQUIRY.

PREPARED BY

CHARLES PHILIP BROWN,

MADRAS CIVIL SERVICE, MEMBER OF THE COLLEGE BOARD, TELUGU TRANSLATOR TO GOVERNMENT, &c.

MADRAS:

PRINTED BY REUBEN TWIGG, AT THE CHRISTIAN KNOWLEDGE SOCIETY'S PRESS, CHURCH STREET, VEPERY.

1850.

PREFACE.

THOSE who have had occasion to transact business with Hindus, or to translate documents written by them, often feel the want of a Key to the various dates in use. For instance: a letter written in A.D. 1822 is dated on "new moon, in [the month] Vaisakh, in [the year bearing the Title] Chitrabhan." The Telugu newspapers now printed at Madras use the same method: Thus; "13th of the bright fortnight in the month Sravana in the year Saumya:"—which is equivalent to 1st August 1849. Even in more important documents the Cyclic Title of the year is always given: but the numeral is generally omitted. In a memoir of Hyder and Tippoo, lately translated from Mahratta, every year is specified by its Cyclic Title alone. All Hindus know by tradition that Hyder's final plundering excursion began in the year "Sarvari" (A.D. 1780) but no numeral is mentioned.

This is not occasioned by ignorance or a neglect of numeration. The Hindus use various methods in recording time. Some dates are numerical. Thus A.D. 1850 answers to the 4951st year of the KALI Yugam or Hindu date of the Creation of the world. The same year is (Title Sa'dharana) 1772-3 of the SALIVAHANA Era: beginning on 14th March in the Telugu countries: on 12th April in the Tamil lands. It is year 1907-8, of the VICRAMA'DITYA Era; beginning in the Guzerat country, on 5th November: elsewhere on 14th March. It is year 1025-26 (beginning 15th September) of the PARASURAMA or COLLAM (Quilon) Era used in Malayalam. And it is year 1266-7 of the HEJRI Era beginning on 6th November.

All these are lunar years: using intercalations to adjust time to the Solar reckoning. Such adjustments cannot be noticed in Chronological tables. The FASLY is a mere official year, beginning on 14th July. It is not divided into months.

Tabular statements of contemporary years *in the last two* centuries have been printed in English by Colonel Warren in his laborious and accurate English volume called 'Ka'la Sankalita: and these are copied in Prinsep's Useful Tables.

In A.D. 1821 the Bramins in the Madras College, encouraged by the English, began to print Sanscrit Almanacks, as they have done in every year since, in the Telugu and Tamil characters: chiefly for astrological purposes: the English dates are also specified: and these manuals have a rapid sale throughout Southern India. But no Chronological Tables have ever been framed by Bramins.

All their calculations in astronomy and chronology are founded on the Kali Yugam: which begins B.C. 3101. Thus A.D. 1850 is A.K. 4951. Like the Julian system invented by Scaliger, this is a mere element in computation: never used in ordinary business. [See page 63.]

In historical inscriptions the Salivahana Sacam (expressed by SS.) is generally employed. Who Salivahana was, or how this era originated, cannot be ascertained: though there are several fables on the subject. Royal grants of land engraven on rocks are found scattered throughout Southern India: and generally are dated according to this era. To Chronologists it is indispensable, but it has now fallen into disuse, and is not always even mentioned in the native Almanacks

The Titular system alone continues in daily use It has certainly lasted for about two thousand years. In this the years are divided into sixties: and every year of the sixty has a different Title. The first year in every cycle has the Title Prabhava: the next is called Vibhava: and the sixtieth is Axaya; after which the next year is Prabhava, beginning a new Cycle. This list of Titles is daily repeated backwards and forwards in every Hindu school, along with the names of the months. But in English schools, Hindu lads are allowed to forget this list: and they therefore will find the tables now printed, a convenient aid in business.

This system is used in India, in Ceylon, and throughout China.* It is the Brihaspati Sacam or Cycle of Jupiter: and learned dissertations on it may be seen in the Asiatic Researches† vol. 3, and in the Kala Sankalita.

The Cyclic system has clearly determined several dates: particularly such as were obscured by error. Thus I found one inscription by a raja named Sri Ranga Rayal, dated Chitrabhanu, SS. 1540. Now this title shews that we must read 1504; and at that time this raja was living. Such errors do not exist in the original marbles: only in the transcripts.

While preparing the present volume I often felt the want of tables shewing the corresponding days in each month during a century past. I therefore employed a learned native astronomer, who has framed an Ephemeris for the century beginning in A.D. 1750. This is printed in a separate volume of 600 pages.

For many ages it has been the custom to quote the Salivahana years by wrong numerals. The SS. 1119 is named Pingala: and yet the same name in some inscriptions is given to 1118. The next year Kalayucti is SS. 1120: yet on some marbles it is written 1124: and the following year Siddharti instead of 1121 becomes 1120. The name Paridhavi belongs to 1654. Yet on some stones it is dated 1653, on others 1655. The year Prajotpatti (A.D. 1811) instead of 1733 is written 1732. Then, two years later, Srímukha 1735 becomes 1736.

It is the custom among Hindus to lay a stress on the Title of a year: while they set little store by its numeral. In every chronological investigation we must satisfy ourselves as to the Title of the year: in most dates the numeral varies one or two years: sometimes five or six years. Even in Almanacks of recent date we find the same easy indifference to numerals. Thus the manuscript Telugu Almanac for the year Vicriti (A.D. 1830) is in some books numbered SS. 1752, in others 1751, and elsewhere 1753. In recording events, the Hindus are vigilant regarding the Title, month, lunation, day, hour and minute: but they care little for accuracy in the numeral of the year.

It would be idle to attribute this deviation, which pervades hundreds of dates, to ignorance. The inscriptions were evidently framed by sound scholars: and mere errors in copying will furnish no explication of fluctuations so universal.

In the tables appended to Warren's Kala Sancalita, the Bramin astronomer who was employed has added foot notes, stating that the year was called in one treatise by one Title: and in another treatise by the next Title. But this solution is of no avail. For he represents the deviation as peculiar to a set of fifteen years in each cycle: whereas it pervades nearly every year: he makes the error always plus, whereas it is as often minus. He makes its quantity only one year: whereas it often is three or even six years. And finally the authorities he quotes are fictitious: for the books he names were written some centuries before the dates which he records.

In the *earlier part* of these tables I have marked the first column (the A.D.) as *Probable*. For we have no means of establishing the precise year in this reckoning which answers to a Hindu date.

The Titles truly appertaining to each year are given in a table now printed (page 33-50) and these tally exactly with so many ancient records that there is no room for doubt. In the Cyclic Tables (page 1-24) many years appear to have no variation. But were the whole of the inscriptions perused most of these years would exhibit discrepancies.

A perusal of manuscripts written in Sanscrit Kannadi Telugu and Tamil has furnished me with the various names of Rajahs that appear in these pages. The Inscriptions usually record little more than donations of land, granted to various individuals, and these have long since become void annulled either by the Musulman invasion, or by Time that greatest of revolutionists.

The Tables commence with A.D. 967. Earlier occurrences are noticed in page 59.

To aid the reader in finding the numeral of any Title that may occur, two tables are given (pages 26-27) of which one gives the SS. numeral: and the other shews the place of the same year according to the European method.

To facilitate the discovery of any Hindu or Musulman name according to date, an Index (page

* The Chinese era of sixty years is described in Rees's Cyclopædia under the word Cycle. It appears that A.D. 1723 is the fortieth year of the seventy-fourth cycle. Now according to the Indian method A.D. 1723 is the thirty-seventh year of the eightieth cycle. And the fortieth year of the seventy-fourth cycle is A.D. 1366. This great difference shews that the two reckonings are wholly separate, though they may have originated in the same system.

† The Asiatic Researches were printed correctly in Calcutta: and lately in French in Paris: but the London octavo Edition "printed verbatim" is very incorrect.

28) is given pointing out the years (A.D.) for eight centuries.

This is followed by a table of three Æras: framed by a native astronomer; wherein every year in the Kali Yugam is assigned its equivalent year according to the Salivahana and Christian reckonings: as also its Title.

Some of the dates of the Salivahana Æra are stated in enigmatical phrases. These are explained in page 51. And this is followed by a notice of the names that occur in the Hindu Zodiac.

The Genealogies of the ancient houses (page 54) are next to be considered. Few of the rajas were able to trace their ancestors for four hundred years: but they usually endeavour to prove themselves sons of the heroes and demi-gods of fabulous ages. I have considered it sufficient to print seven lists which may elucidate the Tables. But many more remain among the Mackenzie records: some were printed by Dr. Francis [Buchanan] Hamilton: in a volume which I never saw.

The general result of my enquiries shews that few Genealogies, more than five centuries old, are worthy of credit; and even the later are not always faultless in dates. It has also been shewn that the oldest existing volumes in the Telugu language are dated after the year one thousand one hundred of the Christian era: at which period the worship of Vishnu was introduced in the Telugu country: and was patronized by a raja who took the name Vishnu Vardhana.

After the year A. D. 1590 we frequently meet with dates according to the Musulman reckoning. From that time therefore the Hejri year has been duly noticed: and after the year A.D. 1630 the Fasly year is also given. Some remarks on these, with the eras used in Bengal, are given in page 63.

In this enquiry I was led to notice a variety of frauds, some historical and some literary: remarks on which (page 65) close the essay.

It remains to notice the sources whence I have collected the facts compressed in this volume.

Lieut. Colonel Colin Mackenzie was Surveyor General of India: he died on 8th May 1821, aged sixty-eight. He had passed many years in collecting materials for a History of India.*

The library accumulated by Mackenzie was purchased by Government. Of his manuscript volumes those portions which consisted of books written in Canarese Telugu Tamil Malayalam and Maharatta were lodged in the College at Madras. Mackenzie had caused translations of many historical tracts to be prepared in English. These were sent to the East India House, and the originals alone were left at Madras.

Being in London in the year 1837 I found another collection of similar manuscripts, chiefly written on palm leaves, in the East India House library, where they lay useless. Of these I wrote a catalogue. In consequence of a notice which I printed on the subject, the whole hoard was in 1844 transmitted to Madras. There I arranged the volumes in the College library along with a large collection made by myself: adding all the volumes (formerly placed in the Literary Society's shelves) that had belonged to Mackenzie. I then caused catalogues to be framed by learned natives; each catalogue is written in the original tongue: but no list has been prepared in English. In examining the store I found many volumes filled with historical Inscriptions. Nearly all of these were in Sanscrit; and they were chiefly written in the Canarese character.

The volumes collected by Colonel Mackenzie are chiefly written on country paper, which the worms are rapidly destroying, while the country ink made of lampblack never fades. A few volumes are written on English paper, but the blackness of English ink soon fades and the writing is in many places nearly illegible. I have therefore caused copies to be made on English paper with country ink. But the work of thus transcribing every volume would cost a sum which I am not ready to lay out on the business.

Some of these had already been partially described in various papers printed in the Madras Journal. But nothing had been done towards a systematic examination.

In the year 1828 Dr. H. H. Wilson (since created Sanscrit professor at Oxford) printed at Calcutta a Descriptive Catalogue of the Mackenzie Collection in two volumes. This learned and perspicuous work encouraged me to commence the study of the Inscriptions: these were numerous. Wilson reckons them more than seven thousand five hundred in number. Another collection of Inscriptions made by Mr. Walter Elliot, containing about seven hundred: and a third procured by that zealous antiquarian Captain Newbold, containing about three hundred, also came into my hands.

Of the records thus perused, the greater part afforded no useful information, beyond that regard-

* Memoirs of Mackenzie have been published in the Journal of the Royal Asiatic Society, (vol 1, page 333-364.) Also in the Asiatic Journal, Dec. 1821, page 537: a brief account is also given in the Saturday Magazine for June 1834, page 242.

ing the date when a particular raja reigned. But as I proceeded, every document was arranged according to dates. In the original volumes no arrangement was attempted, excepting in Mr. Elliot's copy.

I have gone sufficiently far in the enquiry to satisfy my curiosity regarding the successive rulers of the Kannadi and Telugu countries. The inscriptions written in Tamil and Malayalam have been of little avail, because they do not always use the common reckonings (Kali or Salivahana,) but introduce a mode of counting which has not as yet been clearly explained.

In completing the Cyclic Tables I have added, in the margin, notices of some occurrences described in works already published. But most of the statements are original, and are grounded on manuscript authorities.

TABLE OF CONTENTS.

CYCLIC TABLES,

EXPLAINING THE DATES USED IN

HINDU AND MAHOMEDAN CHRONOLOGY

REGARDING THE

HISTORY OF THE TELUGU AND CANARESE COUNTRIES

PREPARED BY C. P. BROWN,

MADRAS CIVIL SERVICE,

TELUGU TRANSLATOR TO GOVERNMENT, &c.

A. D.	Sálivàhana Sacam.		Title.	Notes.
Proba-ble.	True.	*Variation.*		
967	889		1 Prabhava	Contractions of Sanscrit epithets used in these Ta-
968	890		2 Vibhava	bles.
969	891		3 S'ucla	S. Srī *meaning* 'His Grace.'
970	892		4 Pramódúta	D. Dēva 'Noble.'
971	893		5 Prajótpatti	M. Maha 'Great.'
972	894		6 A'ngi'rasa	R. Raja, Raya, Rāyalu. 'Prince, King, Baron.'
973	895		7 Srímukha	P. Pratāpa 'Illustrious.'
974	896		8 Bháva	N. Náyac Lord.
975	897		9 Yuva	V. Vīra Honorable.
976	898		10 Dhátu	Chac. Chacravarti, Emperor.'
977	899		11 I's'wara	
978	900		12 Bahudhánya	
979	901		13 Pramádi	
980	902		14 Vicrama	Kālachurya Chac. R. Murāri-Sovi D, ruler of Kalyā-
981	903		15 Vishu	nam, capital of (Soonda) the Koontala Désam.
982	904		16 Chitrabhánu	
983	905		17 Swabhánu	
984	906		18 Tárana	
985	907		19 Pārthiva	Year 4086 of the KALI ÆRA.
986	908		20 Vyaya	
987	909		21 Sarvajit	Year 377 of the HEJIRA.
988	910		22 Sarvadhárì	Banavasí, a city in the Sunda country, was ruled by
989	911		23 Viródhi	Tailapa D, son of VRD, who was son of Kāma
990	912		24 Vicriti	DR.
991	913		25 Khara	
992	914		26 Nandana	
993	915		27 Vijaya	These two Titles frequently change places.
994	916	/915	28 Jaya	
995	917		29 Manmatha	Káláchurya Bhuja Bala Chacravarti, Murári Sódi DR.
996	918		30 Durmukhi	Note regarding the column of Variations.
997	919		31 Hévilambi	Usually the Titles are quoted correctly, according
998	920		32 Vilambi	to the regular SS. numeral : but occasionally the
999	921		33 Vicári	numeral varies.
1000	922		34 Sárvari	
1001	923		35 Plava	Year 100 of the KOLLAM ÆRA.

A. D.	Sáliváhana Sacam.		Title.	Notes.
Proba-ble.	True.	*Variation.*		
1002	924		36 Subhacrit	Year of Kali Yugam 4102.
1003	925		37 Sóbhacrit	Trailókya Malla R.
1004	926		38 Kródhi	
1005	927		39 Visvávas	
1006	928		40 Parábhava	
1007	929		41 Plavanga	
1008	930		42 Kílaca	End of reign of Tailapa D.
1009	931		43 Saumya	
1010	932		44 Sádháraná	
1011	933		45 Viródhicrit	Vicramáditya, son of Dasavarma.
1012	934		46 Parídhávi	
1013	935		47 Pramádícha	
1014	936		48 A′nanda	SV Gajapati Gaud′éswara.
1015	937		49 Ráxasa	
1016	938		50 Nala	First year of the CHA′LUK-YA Æra: commencing with Bizzana D. in SS. 938, year Nala. His titles are Káláchurya Chacravarti, Jaya Simha D. Tribhuvana Malla; or, Jagad E′ca Malla. His son was Kákati Prólu Ráz. At this time Alanandana Chacravarti ruled S′ri S′ailam.
1017	939		51 Pingala	
1018	940		52 Kálayucti	
1019	941		53 Siddhárthi	
1020	942		54 Raudri	
1021	943		55 Durmati	
1022	944		56 Dundubhi	
1023	945		57 Rudiródgári	
1024	946		58 Ractáxi	
1025	947		59 Kródhana	
1026	948		60 Xaya	This is often spelt Axaya, Acshaya.
1027	949		1 Prabhava	Cycle LXIX commences.
1028	950		2 Vibhava	Tribhuvana Malla's younger brother Trailókya Malla ruled Kalyána Puram.
1029	951		3 S′ucla	
1030	952		4 Pramódúta	First year of Tailapa D. that is, Chá-luk-ya Trailókya Malla.
1031	953		5 Prajótpatti	
1032	954		6 A′ngi′rasa	
1033	955		7 Srímukha	
1034	956		8 Bháva	
1035	957		9 Yuva	
1036	958/964		10 Dhátu	
1037	959		11 I′s′wara	
1038	960		12 Bahudhánya	
1039	961		13 Pramádi	Tailapa D.
1040	962		14 Vicrama	The Tirupati [Tripetty] temples were built.
1041	963		15 Vishu	
1042	964		16 Chitrabhánu	
1043	965		17 Swabhánu	
1044	966		18 Tárana	
1045	967		19 Pārthiva	
1046	968		20 Vyaya	Jayanti was ruled by Tribhuvana Malla: while Siddhavatam was ruled by his brother Trailókya Malla.
1047	969		21 Sarvajit	Year 4148 of the KALI-YUGA.
1048	970		22 Sarvadhári	
1049	971		23 Viródhi	
1050	972		24 Vicriti	
1051	973		25 Khara	
1052	974		26 Nandana	Bhúlóca Malla.
1053	975		27 Vijaya	A′hava Malla D.
1054	976		28 Jaya	Hejira year 416.
1055	977		29 Manmatha	
1056	978		30 Durmukhi	
1057	979		31 Héyilambi	

A. D.	Sáliváhana Sacam.	Title.	Notes.
Probable.	True. *Variation.*		
1058	980	32 Vilambi	Nandana R.
1059	981	33 Vicári	Year 4160 of the Kali Æra.
1060	982	34 Sárvari	
1061	983	35 Plava	The celebrated reformer Sancarachari flourished.
			Trailokya Malla, Jagadeca Malla, Tribhuvana Malla. These three merely mean Lord of the Universe. They are names, apparently of father, son and grandson ; but which is which is not clear.
1062	984	36 Subhacrit	
1063	985	37 Sóbhacrit	
1064	986	38 Kródhi	Tribh. Malla is succeeded by Trailo: Malla.
1065	987/991	39 Visvávas	
1066	988	40 Parábhava	A Solar Eclipse. A great Comet.
1067	989	41 Plavanga	
1068	990	42 Kílaca	Trailōkya Malla ruled Siddhavatam. His elder brother was Tribhuvana Malla.
1069	991	43 Saumya	Tailapa minister (probably) Tribhu. Malla ruled Banavasi.
1070	992	44 Sádháraná	
1071	993	45 Viródhicrit	
1072	994	46 Parídhávi	
1073	995	47 Pramádícha	
1074	996	48 A'nanda	
1075	997	49 Ráxasa	Tailapa R. son of Chāluky R.
1076	998	50 Nala	Kīrti Varma D.?
1077	999	51 Pingala	
1078	1000	52 Kálayucti	Bhuja Bala V. Nārāyana was minister under A'hava Malla.
1079	1001	53 Siddhárthi	
1080	1002	54 Raudri	
1081	1003/1004	55 Durmati	KALI Æra 4182.
1082	1004	56 Dundubhi	
1083	1005	57 Rudiródgári	
1084	1006	58 Ractáxi	
1085	1007	59 Kródhana	
1086	1008	60 Xaya	Ten Malei Pāndya Vannien ruled Sivagiri.
1087	1009	1 Prabhava	Beginning of Cycle LXX.
1088	1010	2 Vibhava	V. Bhadra R. son of Hari Hara D. MDR. This is taken from an inscription in the Telugu language.
1089	1011/1008	3 S'ucla	
1090	1012	4 Pramódúta	
1091	1013/1110	5 Prajótpatti	Nārāyana A'hava Malla.
			From this year until SS. 1070 Orangallu was ruled by Pratápa Rudra D.
1092	1014	6 A'ngi'rasa	
1093	1015	7 Srímukha	HAISANA or HOISANA Erayanga D.
1094	1016	8 Bháva	
1095	1017	9 Yuva	Mallala D.
1096	1018	10 Dhátu	
1097	1019/1020	11 I's'wara	
1098	1020/1021	12 Bahudhánya	Bizzala (or Vijjala, or Bijjana) DR.
1099	1021	13 Pramádi	
1100	1022	14 Vicrama	Rāmānujāchāri eminent Vishnava Reformer.
1101	1023	15 Vishu	
1102	1024	16 Chitrabhánu	The Chola Kings attacked the Chá-luk-ya rājas.
1103	1025	17 Swabhánu	
1104	1026	18 Tárana	
1105	1027	19 Pārthiva	
1106	1028	20 Vyaya	
1107	1029/1030	21 Sarvajit	

A. D.	Sálivâhana Sacam.		Title.	Notes.
Probable.	True.	*Variation.*		
1108	1030		22 Sarvadhári	Vicrama Chóla DMR.
1109	1031		23 Viródhi	
1110	1032		24 Vicriti	Nārāyana Chac. of the Yādava family.
1111	1033		25 Khara	VISHNU VARDHANA, HOISALA, a Chóla king of the Chālukya race; he ruled Rajahmandry on the Godavari; capital of the Vēgi or Vēngī country. The Chálukyas seem to have been Jainas by religion: of the Yadu or Yādava race.
1112	1034		26 Nandana	
1113	1035		27 Vijaya	
1114	1036		28 Jaya	
1115	1037		29 Manmatha	Tribhuvana Malla, who is styled Talaccāḍu Gonga, Bhuja Bala Vīra Ganga.
1116	1038		30 Durmukhi	End of one hundred years of the Cha-luk-ya Dynasty.
1117	1039		31 Hévilambi	
1118	1040		32 Vilambi	First year of Kulōttunga Chola.
1119	1041		33 Vicári	
1120	1042		34 Sárvari	
1121	1043	1042	35 Plava	*Chālukya* Tribhuvana *Malla*, alias Trai-lōk-ya.
1122	1044	1045	36 Subhacrit	
1123	1045		37 Sóbhacrit	Vicrama Chola DMR.
1124	1046		38 Kródhi	Tribhuvana Malla.
1125	1047		39 Visvávas	The Reddis or barons ruled the Telugu country from SS. 1047 until 1361. Beginning of the reign of Chalukya Bhūlōca Malla.
1126	1048		40 Parábhava	
1127	1049		41 Plavanga	
1128	1050	52	42 Kílaca	
1129	1051		43 Saumya	
1130	1052		44 Sádháraná	
1131	1053		45 Viródhicrit	
1132	1054		46 Parídhávi	Dāmalūr in the Guntoor country was ruled by Gonk Arasu. Arasu is the Kannadi word for Rāja.
1133	1055		47 Pramádícha	Bāla Bhāscara Gajapati son of Ganapati.
1134	1056		48 A'nandá	Gajapati Visvambhara D. was crowned. His minister was Gōpa Rāz Rāmanna.
1135	1057		49 Ráxasa	Vijayā ditya came to the throne.
1136	1058		50 Nala	
1137	1059	58	51 Pingala	Accession of Jagad-ēca Malla. Vishnu Vardhana is now styled RR. Narendra.
1138	1060		52 Kálayucti	Gōpu Rāz Rāmanna was *mantri* to the Gajapati Rajas.
1139	1061		53 Siddhárthi	KALI year 4240.
1140	1062		54 Raudri	Accession of Yādava Nārāyana Praudha Pratāpa Chacravarti MDR.
1141	1063		55 Durmati	
1142	1064		56 Dundubhi	
1143	1065		57 Rudiródgári	Vijaya A'ditya R. (See SS. 1057.)
1144	1066	1067	58 Ractáxi	Solar Eclipse. The Vaddeh Rājas called Gajapati-Gaṇapati arose to power.
1145	1067	68/69	59 Kródhana	S'āntala Devi (wife of Vishnu Vardhana) is named as being a Jaina.
1146	1068		60 Xaya	KALI, 4247.
1147	1069		1 Prabhava	Beginning of Cycle LXXI.
1148	1070	71	2 Vibhava	Vishnu Vardhana Yādava: a chief of the Yadu race.
1149	1071		3 S'ucla	Kulōttunga Chola D.
1150	1072		4 Pramódúta	Trailokya Malla Tailapa.
1151	1073		5 Prajótpatti	Gajapati DMR. A'hava Malla R.
1152	1074		6 A'ngi'rasa	Chālukya Tribhuvana Malla.
1153	1075		7 Srímukha	KALI 4254.
1154	1076	77	8 Bháva	V. Vijaya DMPV.

A. D.	Sáliváhana Sacam.	Title.	Notes.
Proba-ble.	True. *Variation.*		
1155	1077	9 Yuva	Siddha MDR. son of Bauddha R.
1156	1078	10 Dhátu	Tribhuvana Malla Bizzana (or VIJJALA) Devar.
1157	1079	11 I′s′wara	Ananta Danda Pāla at Srīcācōlam was succeeded by Sanga R.
1158	1080	12 Bahudhánya	R. Sovi D.
1159	1081	13 Pramádi	The Ballāla barons ruled Orangallu. Bhuja Bala V. Nalla Siddi D. Chola MR. ruled Nelloor.
1160	1082	14 Vicrama	The Lingavant creed is founded by Basava.
1161	1083	15 Vishu	
1162	1084	16 Chitrabhánu	Kalāchūri Chacravarti Tribhuvana Malla D. Mandaleswara Katt Arasu (also called) V. Gonka Arasu.
1163	1085	17 Swabhánu	HOISANA (or, HAISALA) Narasimha D. son of Vishnu Vardhana.
1164	1086	18 Tárana	
1165	1087	19 Pārthiva	
1166	1088	20 Vyaya	BIZZALA (or Vijjala) raja of Banavasi gave certain lands to the Jangams, disciples of Basava.
1167	1089	21 Sarvajit	Kālachurya Chacravarti R. Murāri Sōyi D.
1168	1090	22 Sarvadhári	Deaths of BIZZALA and of Basava.
1169	1091	23 Viródhi	Rāxasa Malla.
1170	1092	24 Vicriti	Kākati-Chacravarti-Kāla-Murāri-Murāri-Sōyi D.
1171	1093	25 Khara	Kulōttunga Chola. Kākatiya Gaṇapati at Chebrolu.
1172	1094/93	26 Nandana	Cālachurya Chacravarti Rāya Murāri Sōyi D.
1173	1095	27 Vijaya	
1174	1096	28 Jaya	
1175	1097	29 Manmatha	Kuntala Desam was ruled by Murāri Sōvi.
1176	1098/99	30 Durmukhi	Accession of A′hava Malla; (alias) Nalla Nissanca Sangama D. Yādava; (alias) Nārāyana Chacravarti.
1177	1099	31 Hévilambi	Chālukya Tribhuvana Malla ruled Banavasi. Sangama D.
1178	1100	32 Vilambi	Kali 4279.
1179	1101	33 Vicári	Tribhuvana Malla Bilvuri Bizzana D.
1180	1102	34 Sárvari	Gonk Arasu. (Arasu means *King*.)
1181	1103/04	35 Plava	Vishnu Vardhana (Hoisala) V. Ballāla D.
1182	1104	36 Subhacrit	Kālachurya Chacr. Sōmēsvara D. son of Trailōkya Malla Nūrmiḍi Tailapa, alias Tribhuvana Malla.
1183	1105	37 Sóbhacrit	
1184	1106	38 Kródhi	
1185	1107	39 Visvávas	V. Ballāla D.
1186	1108	40 Parábhava	V. Nārāyaṇa.
1187	1109	41 Plavanga	
1188	1110	42 Kílaca	I′s′wara D.
1189	1111/13	43 Saumya	
1190	1112	44 Sádháraná	
1191	1113	45 Viródhicrit	Kaddaḍiya Chacr. V. Ballāla D.
1192	1114	46 Parídhávi	Yādava Narayana Bhuja Bala P. Chacr.
1193	1115	47 Pramádícha	
1194	1116/17	48 A′nanda	V. Ballāla D.
1195	1117	49 Ráxasa	
1196	1118	50 Nala	A. H. (that is, Hejira) 593.
1197	1119/1118	51 Pingala	
1198	1120/24	52 Kálayucti	
1199	1121/20	53 Siddhárthi	Sadā Siva, a Jaina by creed. M. Mandalēswara Kārta VD.
1200	1122	54 Raudri	First year of Simhana R. whose minister was Danda Nāyaca. Kārta Vīrya D.
1201	1123	55 Durmati	
1202	1124	56 Dundubhi	V. Ballāla D. Mallapa D. Chacr.
1203	1125	57 Rudiródgári	Bāçaya D Chola MR.

A. D.	Sáliváhana Sacam.	Title.	Notes.
Probable.	True. *Variation.*		
1204	1126/25/27	58 Ractázi	
1205	1127/28	59 Kródhana	Gaṇapati DMR.
1206	1128	60 Xaya	
1207	1129	1 Prabhava	Beginning of Cycle LXXII.
1208	1130/1132	2 Vibhava	Hoisana V. Narasimha.
1209	1131	3 S'ucla	Hoisana V. Ballāla D.
1210	1132	4 Pramódúta	Yādava Narayana P. Chacr. Tribhuvana Malla Singini D. begins his reign.
1211	1133	5 Prajótpatti	Kadamba Chac. of Banavasi.
1212	1134	6 A'ngi'rasa	Bhuja Bala V. Malla DMR. lived about this time.
1213	1135	7 Srímukha	Ganapati DR.
1214	1136	8 Bháva	SMM. Gandá Gópálu Tiru Kālatti D. Chola MR.
1215	1137/27	9 Yuva	A Sanscrit inscription uses the name " Telunga."
1216	1138	10 Dhátu	
1217	1139/40	11 I's'wara	Rama Nārāyana D first year of V. Malli D.
1218	1140	12 Bahudhánya	V. Ballála D.
1219	1141	13 Pramádi	
1220	1142	14 Vićrama	Kādamba Chacr.
1221	1143	15 Vishu	Dēv Arasu.
1222	1144	16 Chitrabhánu	
1223	1145	17 Swabhánu	
1224	1146	18 Tárana	Simhana D.
1225	1147	19 Pārthiva	Siddaiia, Son of DMR ruled Ḳānchi (Conjevaram) and Kākati Gan'apati was his minister. The Kákatí family was of the ' Reddi' or farmer tribe.
1226	1148/47	20 Vyaya	Açça̧la [*Utsulu*] DMR. ruled Vencatageri.
1227	1149	21 Sarvajit	Simhana D.
1228	1150	22 Sarvadhári	Hoisana Vīra Narasimha D.
1229	1151	23 Viródhi	Kali year 4330.
1230	1152	24 Vicriti	End of reign of Kākatí Gaṇapati.
1231	1153	25 Khara	V. Malla D.
1232	1154	26 Nandana	Truk kālita D. Chola MR.
1233	1155	27 Vijaya	Kulóttunga Rājendra Chola.
1234	1156	28 Jaya	Narasimha D.
1235	1157	29. Manmatha	Hoisana V. Ballāla D.
1236	1158	30 Durmukhi	
1237	1159/53	31 Hévilambi	Simhana R. Chalukya Nāráyana Nalla Sidda D. ruled the Vēngī country (*i. e.* Rajahmandry.) Ganda Gōpāla Tiruk Kālita D. Chola MR. ruled Nellore.
1238	1160	32 Vilambi	Kumāra Kākatīya Rudra DMR.
1239	1161	33 Vicári	
1240	1162	34 Sárvari	Simhana R. The Black Pagoda at Jagannath in Orissa was built.
1241	1163	35 Plava	Sōvi DR. Bayya Chola begins to reign. Ganapati R. is succeeded by his son Kākatī Rudra D. who reigned until SS. 1215.
1242	1164	36 Subhacrit	
1243	1165	37 Sóbhacrit	
1244	1166	38 Kródhi	Simhana R.
1245	1167	39 Visvávas	Hari-Hara R. Sōmēswara.
1246	1168	40 Parábhava	
1247	1169	41 Plavanga	Tacc Arasu Gangaiia DMR. Trailókya Malla V. Náráyana ruled Kalyānam.
1248	1170	42 Kílaca	Kali year 4349.
1249	1171	43 Saumya	Year 425 of the Kollam Æra.
1250	1172	44 Sádháraná	
1251	1173	45 Viródhicrit	S. Kannara DR. V. Malla D.
1252	1174	46 Parídhávi	Hoisala Vīra Ballāla D. Kākatī Ganapati D. ruled Orangallu (Warangole.)

A. D.	Sáliváhana Sacam.	Title.	Notes.
Probable.	True. *Variation.*		
1253	1175/81	47 Pramádícha	V. Bukka R.
1254	1176	48 A'nanda	
1255	1177	49 Ráxasa	Eclipse of the Moon.
1256	1178	50 Nala	Kannara D. Gangaiia Sāhini.
1257	1179/71/80	51 Pingala	V. Ballāla D. Ganapati R.
1258	1180	52 Kálayucti	
1259	1181	53 Siddhárthi	Kannara D.
1260	1182	54 Raudri	Kali year 4361. Nīla Kantha Náyac.
1261	1183	55 Durmati	Kākatīya Ganápati. Death of Gaṇḍa Penḍéra Zinniga DMR. Siddaiia D.
1262	1184	56 Dundubhi	Tripur-āntaca DR. son of Chola R.
1263	1185/81	57 Rudiródgári	Dēv ālw' ēndra.
1264	1186	58 Ractáxi	V. Ballāla D.
1265	1187	59 Króḍhana	MRM. Ganḍa Gōpāla Tiruk Kāllatti D. Chola MR.
1266	1188	60 Xaya	Ganḍa Penḍēra Murāri Narayana Bramha Raxasa Zannaiia DMR. ruled Kanchi. Kākatīya Rudra D.
1267	1189	1 Prabhava	Beginning of Cycle LXXIII.
1268	1190	2 Vibhava	MDR. Kākatī Pratāpa Rudra D. ruled Orangolu from SS. 1190 until 1241.
1269	1191/92	3 S'ucla	Vishnu Vardhana is placed by some in this year : but more correctly in SS. 1103.
1270	1192	4 Pramódúta	Bramha Raxasa Tripur ántaca DMR. Zannaiia DMR. First year of Yādava-Nārāyana-Praudha-Pratāpa-Chacravarti-S-Rama-chandra-D.
1271	1193/94	5 Prajótpatti	Solar Eclipse.
1272	1194/95	6 A'ngi'rasa	Hoisana V. Narasimha D. at Dwāra-Samudram.
1273	1195	7 Srímukha	Ambi D. V. Rama Chandra D.
1274	1196/97	8 Bháva	
1275	1197/96	9 Yuva	Dēvanna Amritaiia.
1276	1198	10 Dhátu	Rama Chandra D.
1277	1199	11 I's'wara	Kākatī Pratápa Rudra DMR. Ganápatí MR. From SS. 1199 until SS. 1299 the *Reddi Vāru* ruled the Telugu country.
1278	1200	12 Bahudhánya	Hoisana Narasimha D. The Black Pagoda at Jagannath was completed.
1279	1201	13 Pramádi	Rāja-nagar, afterwards called Rājamahendri was ruled by V. Chola MR. younger son of Rājendra Chola ; whose son Rāja Rāz abdicated in favour of his younger brother this V. Chola.
1280	1202	14 Vicrama	Kali 4381 Trailōkya Malla DR.
1281	1203	15 Vishu	Pōlaia Reddi ruled Kondavīḍu.
1282	1204/03	16 Chitrabhánu	Rama Chandra DR. of the Yādava race.
1283	1205	17 Swabhánu	Ranga RMR.
1284	1206	18 Tárana	Hoisana V. Narasimha D. Rama Chandra D.
1285	1207	19 Pārthiva	Kali year 4386.
1286	1208	20 Vyaya	Sōmana ruled A'négondi. In this year Hari Hara R. was succeeded by Praudha R.
1287	1209/07/08/10	21 Sarvajit	Hoisana V. Narasimha D. Bramha Rāxasa-Ganda-Pendēra-Amba-DR ruled Gandicōṭa, &c.
1288	1210	22 Sarvadhári	V. Narasimha D. Yādava R.
1289	1211/12	23 Viródhi	Rāma Chandra D.
1290	1212	24 Vicriti	The Orangolu princes ruled Chicacolu from SS. 1081 until 1213. And from SS. 1214 till 1273, Kākatī Pratapa Rudra DR. ruled Chicacolu. He was of the Reddi caste. This Rudra Deva is the person called by Ferishta "Ludder Deo." He ruled Ecasila nagar, or Orangólu. *i. e.* Wanṭimitta.
1291	1213/12	25 Khara	Nandana Chacravarti.

A. D.	Sálivábana Sacam.	Title.	Notes.
Proba-ble.	True. *Variation.*		
1292	1214	26 Nandana	End of the reign of Sri-Kumāra-Kākatīya-Pratāpa-Ganapati-Rudra-D. who ruled Chicacolu for 51 years.
1293	1215/16	27 Vijaya	The Musulmans (Pathans) descended from Delhi: they conquered Rajahmandri and Kulbarga.
1294	1216/15	28 Jaya	Hejri year 694.
1295	1217	29 Manmatha	Ballāla D. whom Ferishta (Briggs. 1. 373) calls Bilal Dew. Sōyi D.
1296	1218/20	30 Durmukhi	Anapōtu Reddi.
1297	1219/15	31 Hévilambi	
1298	1220	32 Vilambi	Mandēla-Bramha-Raxasa-Pendera-Amba DMR.
1299	1221	33 Vicári	The Black Pagoda in Orissa was completed.
1300	1222/20/24	34 Sárvari	A great eclipse of the moon at full.
1301	1223	35 Plava	
1302	1224/23	36 Subhacrit	
1303	1225	37 Sóbhacrit	
1304	1226/27	38 Kródhi	Mandēla Bramha-Raxasa-Ganda-Pendēra-Tripurāri D.
1305	1227/28	39 Visvávas	Hari Hara R. of Vijaya-nagar died. He was succeeded by his son Praudha D.
1306	1228	40 Parábhava	The Pathans conquered Deoghur.
1307	1229	41 Plavanga	Ana Vema Reddi. The Reddis were feudal chiefs of the agricultural caste.
1308	1230/31	42 Kílaca	
1309	1231	43 Saumya	
1310	1232	44 Sádháraná	
1311	1233	45 Viródhicrit	Kali year 4412.
1312	1234	46 Parídhávi	The Musulmans had now taken all the Telugu countries and invaded the Tamil countries.
1313	1235/36	47 Pramádícha	Chicca Vadeyar, minister of Chola Raz. R. Zuṭṭu Ellanca Gonka Reddi; son of Pratapa Rudra.
1314	1236	48 A'nanda	Pratapa V. Bhanu D.
1315	1237	49 Ráxasa	
1316	1238	50 Nala	V. Ballala R.
1317	1239	51 Pingala	
1318	1240	52 Kálayucti	Kumāra Kākatíya Pratāpa Rudra D. continues to rule Orangallu [Wantimitta] from SS. 1190 to 1242 or 1245. In his days the Bhascara Ramayan was written. There were, in succession five Vaddeh Reddis, named, 1 Polaya (or Prōli) Vema Reddi ruled Duggirala in the Palnáḍu country. 2 Anavōtu Reddi ruled for 30 years. 3 His younger brother Ana Vema Reddi. 4 Kumāra giri Reddi. 5 Rāça Vema Reddi.
1319	1241	53 Siddhárthi	
1320	1242	54 Raudri	
1321	1243	55 Durmati	
1322	1244	56 Dundubhi	Kulōttunga Chola.
1323	1245	57 Rudiródgári	Beginning of reign of Harihara Razu who ruled until 1257.
1324	1246	58 Ractáxi	
1325	1247	59 Kródhana	
1326	1248	60 Xaya	
1327	1249/1250	1 Prabhava	Cycle LXXIV commences.
1328	1250	2 Vibhava	Praudha DR. is succeeded by his son Vijaya DR.
1329	1251/1250	3 S'ucla	
1330	1252	4 Pramódúta	

A. D.	Sálivâhana Sacam.		Title.	Notes.
Probable.	True.	*Variation.*		
1331	1253		5 Prajótpatti	Vidyāranya Swami wrote the Commentaries on the Vedas.
1332	1254		6 A'ngi'rasa	Kali 4433.
1333	1255		7 Srímukha	Trailokya Natha D.
1334	1256		8 Bháva	Manu-maya D. Choda MR: son of Bramhaya D.
1335	1257		9 Yuva	Ganapati Pratapa Rudra Deva was succeeded by his son Krishna Rao ? ?
1336	1258		10 Dhátu	Hari Hara R. son of A'rvét'i Bukka Raza (alias SVP. DMR.) of the Golla (herdsmen) caste.
1337	1259		11 I's'wara	
1338	1260		12 Bahudhánya	S. Ranga RMK.
1339	1261		13 Pramádi	Praudha DR. Proli Reddi ruled (Kundiní Patnam) Condavīdu.
1340	1262		14 Vicrama	He is succeeded by Véma Reddi.
1341	1263		15 Vishu	The Musulmans from the North invade the Southern districts [Deccan.]
1342	1264		16 Chitrabhánu	
1343	1265		17 Swabhánu	Kali 4444.
1344	1266		18 Tárana	
1345	1267		19 Pārthiva	Vira Kampen'a Vadéyar.
1346	1268/1270		20 Vyaya	DRMR.
1347	1269		21 Sarvajit	Tribhuvana Malla. Dowlatabad and Warangolu were ruled by Ein ul Mulk, under Sūltan Mahomed Toghlak. While Bidar (Beedur, Bednore) and Kalbarga were ruled by Ala-ud-Din. This was the title assumed in AD. 1345 by Nizam Bhair governor of Sambal. He was killed in this year.
1348	1270		22 Sarvadhári	
1349	1271		23 Viródhi	Kali 4450.
1350	1272/1270		24 Vicriti	VS. A'rvét'i Bukka Rāyal (the Golla or herdsman) succeeded his father Hari Hara Rāyal at A'négondi.
1351	1273		25 Khara	
1352	1274		26 Nandana	
1353	1275		27 Vijaya	Mummadi Naik Reddi: apparently the grandfather of Mummadi Praudha Rāyalu.
1354	1276		28 Jaya	
1355	1277		29 Manmatha	
1356	1278/1279		30 Durmukhi	
1357	1279		31 Hévilambi	
1358	1280		32 Vilambi	SV. Bukka Vadeyar and Vema Reddi and V. Bhadra Reddi; ruled Rajahmandry.
1359	1281		33 Vicári	Kali 4460.
1360	1282		34 Sárvari	Vijayanagar (Beejnugr) was ruled by Pratāpa V. Gaudēswara; also called Pratapa Kapilés'wara.
1361	1283		35 Plava	Prolu was ruled by Anavótu Vema Reddi ; Vidyā nagar was ruled by Vidyāranya Swamulu. He was succeeded in SS. 1284 by ŚV. Bukka R. who ruled Hastināpuram.
1362	1284		36 Subhacrit	
1363	1285/1286		37 Sóbhacrit	
1364	1286		38 Kródhi	
1365	1287		39 Visvávas	
1366	1288		40 Parábhava	
1367	1289		41 Plavanga	
1368	1290		42 Kílaca	
1369	1291		43 Saumya	Mohammad Shah Bahmini (the first) invaded the Deccan and conquered Vijayanagar.
1370	1292/1293		44 Sádháraná	Man'avála M. Muni the Hindu Saint, the disciple of Bhashya Carlu.

A. D.	Sálivάhana Sacam.	Title.	Notes.
Proba-ble.	True. *Variation.*		
1371	1293	45 Viródhicrit	Praudha DR ?
1372	1294	46 Parídhávi	Bukka R. son of Hari'hara R. ruled Vijàyanagar.
1373	1295	47 Pramádícha	
1374	1296	48 A'nanda	Mohammad Shah Bahmini (the first) after ruling 17 years was succeeded by Mujahid Shah. Briggs's Translation of Ferishta, 2. 328.
1375	1297	49 Ráxasa	
1376	1298/1297	50 Nala	DR. Kali 4476.
1377	1299/1300	51 Pingala	
1378	1300/1299	52 Kálayucti	Mujahid Khan was succeeded by Daood Khan Bahmini ; who was soon murdered : and was succeeded by Mahmood Shah Bahmini.
1379	1301	53 Siddhárthi	
1380	1302	54 Raudri	
1381	1303	55 Durmati	Harihara R. son of Bukka Paya
1382	1304/1305	56 Dundubhi	
1383	1305	57 Rudiródgári	Harihara R. is succeeded by his son Praudha DR ?
1384	1306	58 Ractâxi	
1385	1307	59 Kródhana	Harihara R. whose minister was Bhavadūru Odayar
1386	1308	60 Xaya	
1387	1309	1 Prabhava	Cycle 75th begins.
1388	1310/1312	2 Vibhava	
1389	1311	3 S'ucla	Kali 4490. Hejri. 792.
1390	1312/13/15	4 Pramódúta	Ellanka Gonka Reddi son of Pratápa Rudra.
1391	1313	5 Prajótpatti	
1392	1314/13/15	6 A'ngi'rasa	Deva Raya, (or) Praudha DR. son of Hari Hara R. ruler of Vijayanagar. Kātam Reddi Vēma Reddi at Pithápuram.
1393	1315/16/17	7 Srímukha	Kathāri Sālava Narasimha R. son of Narasinga R. Vallabha R.
1394	1316/15/17	8 Bháva	
1395	1317	9 Yuva	
1396	1318/1319	10 Dhátu	The Durga Dēvī Xāmam ; a famine that lasted twelve years and ruined the country between the Godavari and the Krishna. Duff. 1. 59.
1397	1319	11 I's'wara	Ganga D. ruler of Chōla.
1398	1320	12 Bahudhánya	Devala R. of Vijayanagar invaded Kalbarga ?
1399	1321	13 Pramádi	SVPDRMR. Ferishta gives long details regarding this ' Deo Rāya.'
1400	1322	14 Vicrama	Kali 4501. SVDR Wadeyar ruled Udayagiri.
1401	1323/22/24/26	15 Vishu	
1402	1324	16 Chitrabhánu	
1403	1325/1326	17 Swabhánu	DRMR.
1404	1326/1327	18 Tárana	Harihara R. Vēma Reddi ruled the Vēngi (or Vēgi) country.
1405	1327/1326	19 Pārthiva	SV. Bukka. R.
1406	1328/1327	20 Vyaya	Vema Reddi's descendants ruled Addanki. DRMR. was besieged in Vijayanagar by Ferozu Shah Bahmini. (Briggs's Fer.) Vema was conquered and compelled to give his daughter in marriage to Feroz Shah.
1407	1329/28/30	21 Sarvajit	Malla Reddi, grandson of Ana Vema Reddi.
1408	1330	22 Sarvadhári	Kali 4509. Hejri 811.
1409	1331/1332	23 Viródhi	Ballāla R. Bukka R. An Eclipse. Hari Hara R. SVPDRMR.
1410	1332/1333	24 Vicriti	Velugōti Gangal R.
1411	1333	25 Khara	
1412	1334	26 Nandana	

A. D.	Sálivâhana Sacam.	Title.	Notes.
Proba-ble.	True. *Variation.*		
1413	1335	27 Vijaya	Malli R.
1414	1336/1330	28 Jaya	
1415	1337/1338	29 Manmatha	Kãtam Reddi Vema Reddi...Praudha Rãyalu.
1416	1338/1339	30 Durmukhi	
1417	1339/1342	31 Hévilambi	Harihara R. is succeeded by his son VPDR. Feroz Shah again attacked DRMR. but was defeated.
1418	1340	32 Vilambi	Vijaya Bukko R. is succeeded by Palla Bukka R.
1419	1341	33 Vicári	DRMR. of Vijayanagar leagues with Krishna R. of Warangolu against Ahmad Shah. Briggs. p. 406.
1420	1342	34 Sárvari	A. Hejri 823.
1421	1343/1342	35 Plava	A grievous famine in the Deccan.
1422	1344	36 Subhacrit	Feroz Shah is succeeded by Ahmad Shah. Death of Bukka Rayal alias SVPDMR. who ruled Vidyanagar for sixty years. His son Harihara DR. and his grandson Praudha DR. are often like him styled merely Deva Raya.
1423	1345	37 Sóbhacrit	
1424	1346	38 Kródhi	
1425	1347	39 Visvávas	Pratãpa Kumãra DMR. ruled Vijáyanagar DRMR.
1426	1348	40 Parábhava	VR. Vadevar.
1427	1349	41 Plavanga	
1428	1350	42 Kílaca	
1429	1351/52/53	43 Saumya	Collam year 604. Kali 4530....A. H. 833.
1430	1352/1353	44 Sádháraná	VPDR. at Vijayanagar. DRMR. son of Vijaya RMR. Timmappa Vadeyar.
1431	1353/1354	45 Viródhicrit	
1432	1354/1353	46 Parídhávi	
1433	1355/44/57	47 Pramádícha	
1434	1356/1357	48 A'nanda	Katam Reddi, Vema Reddi. Komaragri Reddi.
1435	1357/1358	49 Ráxasa	Mummadi Praudha R. ruled Pushpagiri.
1436	1358	50 [illegible]a	SVPDRMR.
1437	1359/1360	51 [illegible]gala	At this time the Musulmans used no fire arms : see A. D. 1510.
1438	1360	52 [illegible]ayucti	Kali 4539....AH. 842. The REDDI'S ruled from SS. 1047 until SS. 1361.
1439	1361	53 Siddhárthi	DRMR. Praudha DR. Narasa R. ruled Anantapuram and Kampti.
1440	1362	54 Raudri	
1441	1363/1364	55 Durmati	
1442	1364/1365	56 Dundubhi	
1443	1365	57 Rudiródgári	PDRMR. of Vijayanagar rebelled against Ala-ud-din Shah : but after three battles was quelled and offered tribute. Fer. 2. 432.
1444	1366	58 Ractáxi	Vira Narasimha Rayalu.
1445	1367	59 Kródhana	
1446	1368/1369	60 Xaya	
1447	1369	1 Prabhava	Cycle LXXVI. commences. At this time there were thirteen independant Mahomedan Kings in India. (Ferishta, IV. 555.)
1448	1370	2 Vibhava	Kapil Endra Gajapati.
1449	1371/1370	3 S'ucla	Immadi DR. Narasa Rayalu is succeeded by Krishna Rayal—not the celebrated one.
1450	1372	4 Pramódúta	Mallic Arjuna R. son of DRMR. also called Mummadi Praudha DR. ruled Vizianagar.
1451	1373	5 Prajótpatti	
1452	1374/1376	6 A'ngi'rasa	War in the Concan between two Musulman chiefs, Fer. 2. 436-448.

A. D.	Sáliváhana Sacam.	Title.	Notes.
Proba-ble.	True. *Variation.*		
1453	1375	7 Srímukha	
1454	1376/1377	8 Bháva	R. Sēkhara R.
1455	1377/1374	9 Yuva	Kali 4556. AH. 859.
1456	1378	10 Dhátu	Sāluva Tirumala DMR. son of Gōpaya DMR. of the Chola realm.
1457	1379/1377	11 I's'wara	V. Pratapa MDR. also called Praudha DR. ruled Penagonda. His son Vijaya DR. ruled Vijayanagar.
1458	1380/1381	12 Bahudhánya	The Musulmans overran the Telugu country but were defeated at Orangolu the capital. (Fer. 2. 529) the title Nizām-ul-Mulk Bhairavi was bestowed by Humayūn on a Hindu proselyte. (Fer. 521.)
1459	1381	13 Pramádi	DRMR. Vijaya Ranga Socca Linga Nayu.
1460	1382	14 Vicrama	S. Mallic Arjuna R. A rebellion by Musulman generals against the Emperor Humayun : who vanquishes them and puts them to death by torture. Fer. 2. 462. He dies and is succeeded by Nizam Shah : against whom the rajas of Orissa and Rajahmandry rebel. Ferishta 2. 466.
1461	1383/1384	15 Vishu	Condapilli was ruled by the Gajapatis who ruled Orissa. Hiriya Bhairava D. ruled Nagar.
1462	1384/1385	16 Chitrabhánu	Sultan Mahmood of Malwa invades Ahmedabad and Bider.
1463	1385	17 Swabhánu	
1464	1386/1387	18 Tárana	Death of Krishna Rayal—not the celebrated prince.
1465	1387/84/88	19 Pārthiva	A petty war in Palnaud by Bramhi Nayudu.
1466	1388	20 Vyaya	Saluva Narasing R. at Vidyānagar.
1467	1389/1390	21 Sarvajit	Virūpāxa R. The Musulmans were scattered through many districts in which as yet they were not fighting.
1468	1390	22 Sarvadhári	
1469	1391	23 Viródhi	
1470	1392	24 Vicriti	Kali 4571. AH. 875.
1471	1393/1394	25 Khara	Virūpāxa DRMR. at Vijayanagar. Mohammad Shah invades the Orissa and Rajahmandri countries. Kathāri Sālava Narasingaiia DMR. ruled Masulipatam, Vijayanagar, &c. Ferish. 2. 498.
1472	1394	26 Nandana	
1473	1395/1397	27 Vijaya	
1474	1396	28 Jaya	A famine for two years in the Telugu [Tellinga, Tylung] country. Ferish. 2. 494.
1475	1397	29 Manmatha	V. Pāndya D. Nalarām S. Ranga R.
1476	1398	30 Durmukhi	S. Ranga R.
1477	1399/1400	31 Hévilambi	
1478	1400/1401	32 Vilambi	Virūp-āxa R.
1479	1401/1402	33 Vicāri	R. Sābini Nāyani Vencatapati Nayudu. Mohammad Shah plundered Conjevaram and Masulipatam which was ruled by Narasinga R.
1480	1402	34 Sárvari	
1481	1403	35 Plava	Virūp-āxa R. Salava Timma Raz. Mallic Arjuna R. Mohammad Shah murdered his prime minister. Ferish. 2. 509.
1482	1404	36 Subhacrit	Siva Raya of Vijayanagar (?) sent an army against Goa.

A. D.	Sálivâhana Sacam.	Title.	Notes.
Proba-ble.	True. *Variation.*		
1483	1405	37 Sóbhacrit	Mohamed Shah Bahmini I. is succeeded by Bahm. II.
1484	1406	38 Kródhi	
1485	1407	39 Visvávas	Feuds arise among the Musulman rulers.
1486	1408/1409	40 Parábhava	Kawam-ul-Mulk *Senior*, (ruler of Rajahmandri) seized Orangolu ; and was slain in a civil war among the courtiers. Finally Nizam-ul-Mulk gained the mastery and became vizier to Mohammad Shah : and appointed Kawam-ul-Mulk *junior*, ruler of Telingana. Then Mahmood Shah ordered Dilāwar Khan to slay all his (the Shah's) viziers.
1487	1409	41 Plavanga	Rama Chandra Rayal.
1488	1410	42 Kílaca	Virūp-āxa R. AH. 894. V. Narasanna R.
1489	1411	43 Saumya.	V. Nanzaiia.
1490	1412	44 Sádháraná	Nizam-ul-Mulk is slain by King Mahmood's order. Virūp-āxa R. is succeeded by Narasinga R. A plot to murder Mahmood Shah. Three days massacre in Bidar-Ahmadabad (Ferisht. 2. 543.) The Sultan's troops are defeated. (ib. p. 586.)
1491	1413	45 Viródhicrit	Kaṭhári Salava Immadi Narasimha DRMR.
1492	1414/1415	46 Parídhávi	At this time no fire arms were in use. Ferish 2. 533.
1493	1415	47 Pramádícha	Sālava Timma Raz is vanquished at (Beejnugr) Vizayanagar by Yūsaf A'dil Khan. Ferish. 3. 12.
1494	1416	48 A'nanda	Condapilli and Bezoada were ruled by Mallaya M. Patrulu.
1495	1417	49 Ráxasa	Sālava Narasinga Raya was succeeded by Narasa R. Sultan Kulli Kutb-ul-Mulk Hamdani was appointed governor of (Orangolu) the Telugu and Golconda countries. Fer. 2. 544.
1496	1418	50 Nala	The Vaddèh Razulu, or Gajapatis began their rule. The first was V. Bhadra Gajapati. The Musulman ruler of Ahmadabad (Bidar) rebelled against the emperor. Fer. 3. 16.
1497	1419/1418	51 Pingala	Civil wars between the Musulman rulers. Fer. 2. 546. and 3. 18. No fire arms.
1498	1420	52 Kálayucti	Narasima DR. at Coilguntla.
1499	1421/1422	53 Siddhárthi	Sālava Immadi Narasimha R. Sālava DR. Vadeyar.
1500	1422	54 Raudri	
1501	1423/22/24	55 Durmati	Kali 4602. Hej. 907. D. Arasu Vadeyar V. Nanja R. SV. Bhairava Vadeyar.
1502	1424	56 Dundubhi	
1503	1425/1424	57 Rudiródgári	Immaḍi Kathari Narsinga Raya.
1504	1426	58 Ractáxi	
1505	1427/1426	59 Kródhana	
1506	1428/1429	60 Xaya	AH. 912. The Musulman have contentions among themselves regarding sects.
1507	1429/1430	1 Prabhava	Cycle LXXVII. Mallic Arjuna R. son of DRMR.
1508	1430/1428	2 Vibhava	Saluva Narsimha R. (a Cshatriya) His minister (a brahman) was Saluva Timmaya. This raja dies and is succeeded by the cęlebrated PV Krishna DR. whose minister was Appājī. Date Magha Suddha 14.
1509	1431/30/32	3 S'ucla	
1510	1432/31/33	4 Pramódúta	Goa was conquered by the Portugueze under Albuquerque. After this date we first meet with mention of cannon and musketry in Indian History.
1511	1433/32/34	5 Prajótpatti	Timmarāz DMR. was raja of the Karnātac and Tulava countries.

A. D.	Sálivâhana Sacam.	TITLE.	NOTES.
Proba-ble.	True. *Variation.*		
1512	1434/32/35	6 A'ngi'rasa	Sultan Kulli Kutb-ul-Mulk (Bri. Fe. 2. 549) rebels against Mahmood Shah Emperor of Delhi. He becomes king of the Telugu country (' Telingana.') A battle at Ahmadabād-Bidar, in which Mahmood was defeated. Bhairava R. Vadeyar.
1513	1435	7 Srímukha	V. Bhadra Gajapati, the last of the Gajapati rajahs of Kalinga and Andhra, was conquered by Krishna R.
1514	1436/35/37	8 Bhāva	(Details of awful cruelties committed by Púsapáṭi Mádhava Varma upon the Velamas.)
1515	1437/35/38	9 Yuva	
1516	1438/1437	10 Dhátu	Vijayanagar was ruled by Sadasiva. And Vinuconda, Kondaviḍu, Bellamconda, Nāgārjana-Konda, Ammanabolu, Addanki, Tangedu, Ketavaram, and Udayagiri were ruled by Pratápa Rudra Gajapati.
1517	1439/1438	11 I's'wara	A Solar Eclipse.... Mir Jumla (Sayad Moham. Zulf-ukkār-Khan) Nawab of Golconda. He was the Vizier of Nawab Abd-ul-Kutb Shah of Golconda.
1518	1440	12 Bahudhānya	Singaia DMR. ruled Udayagiri. Bukka R. Timmaiia DMR. Saluva Timma Raz was minister to Krishna R.
1519	1441/40/44	13 Pramádi	Battle on the banks of the Krishn'a. In this battle Ismael A'dil Shah attacked Krishna Raya, raja of (Bijnagr) Vijayanagar. The Hindus used musquetry and cannon. The Nabob was defeated : and then made peace with Burhan Nazim Shah of Ahmadnagar in May.1544 (Brig. Fer. 3. 50—52.)
1520	1442/1441	14 Vicrama	Kali 4621. Hejri 927. VPD..Rama Chandra D. Virūp-āxa R.
1521	1443	15 Vishu	Krishna Raya expelled the Musulmans. Matla Kona RD. Chōda MR.
1522	1444/1445	16 Chitrabhánu	The two Bramin theologians Appaiia Dīxatlu of Virinchi puram, and Tātachāri lived at this time.
1523	1445/44/46/51	17 Swabhánu	Achyuta Rāyal.
1524	1446	18 Tárana	Timmaiia DR. son of Bukka R.
1525	1447/46/50	19 Pārthiva	V. Rudra Pratāpa D. ruled Katagam (Cuttack.)
1526	1448/46/47	20 Vyaya	
1527	1449/44/51	21 Sarvajit	A. H. 934. Fire arms were scarcely known in India. Ferishta states that in A. D. 1529 they were not used in battle.
1528	1450/47/52	22 Sarvadhari	
1529	1451/1452	23 Viródhi	Death of Krishna Raya. This is the celebrated patron of Allasāni Peddanna. The Tānēshā was reigning.
1530	1452/51/53	24 Vicriti	Achyuta DR. came to the throne and ruled until SS. 1497.
1531	1453/51/54	25 Khara	The Musulman chiefs in the Deccan were at war between themselves.
1532	1454/55/57	26 Nandana	Achyuta DR. ruled Vijayanagar....Achyuta DR. worshipped a god named Channa Raya. These were the last of the Gajapati kings. His ministers were Timmaiia, and Sāluva Horiya Tirumala R. Kandanúl was ruled by Sadāsiva
1533	1455	27 Vijaya	

A. D.	Sâlivâhana Sacam.	Title.	Notes.
Proba-ble.	True. *Variation.*		
1534	1456/1457	28 Jaya	Tirumala Raya invited Ibrahim Adil Shah: persuaded him to depart: and then killed himself. Briggs's Fer. 3. 84. See details there.
1535	1457/1458	29 Manmatha	
1536	1458/55/61	30 Durmukhi	Bukka R. Timmappa DMR.
1537	1459/1460	31 Hévilambi	Bengilūr (Bangalore) was founded.
1538	1460	32 Vilambi	DRMR.
1539	1461/60/62	33 Vicári	Tannasha (Tānīshah, that is, Abdul Hasr, Kutb-ul-mulk, Nabob of Golconda) sent his ministers Akkanna and Mādanna to govern the Telugu country. They appointed Podili Lingappa to rule the districts south of the river Krishna.
1540	1462/1463	34 S'árvari	
1541	1463	35 Plava	Death of Achyuta Ráyalu. He was succeeded by his son Sadā Siva.
1542	1464/66/67	36 S'ubhacrit	
1543	1465/66/67	37 S'óbhacrit	
1544	1466/1464	38 Kródhi	Sadā Siva D. ruled Vijāyanagar. Kathāri Sālava Narasinga R. ruled Orangallu (Wantimetta.)
1545	1467/66/68	39 Vis'vávas	A. H. 952.
1546	1468/64/69	40 Parábhava	
1547	1469/1470	41 Plavanga	The Portugueze settled at Mailapur (Madras) which they called St. Thomé.
1548	1470/1471	42 Kílaca	The Deccan was divided into five realms. A'dil Shah was king of Bījāpūr. Kutb Shah — Golconda Imad Shah — Berar Nizam Shah — Ahmadnagar Bereed Shah — Ahmadābad-Bidar. On these see As. Ann. Reg. 1800 "characters" page 4 note†
1549	1471/70/73	43 Saumya	A. D. Ferishta 3. 183 says "Burhan Nazim Shah leagued with the Raja of Penagonda, and invaded the realm of Ibrahim Adil Shah: they marched to reduce Shahdroog (Srāvana Durgam) and Sholapore: and laid siege to some forts on the frontier of the Carnatic. The Musulmans marched as far as Purendra when they halted because the Raja of Penagonda had not yet begun his march.
1550	1472/71/73	44 Sádháraná	
1551	1473/72/74	45 Viródhicrit	Pemma Sani Timma Nayu built Gandicōṭá. Aliya Rāma Raya (son-in-law to Krishna Raya) succeeds to the throne.
1552	1474/70/76	46 Parídhávi	Up to this period the Inscriptions were in Sanscrit: except a few written in Kanarese. From this time a few occur in Telugu. But Sanscrit is the usual language.
1553	1475/1476	47 Pramádicha	
1554	1476/73/77	48 A'nanda	Erra Rājaiia ruled Kanchi (Conjevaram.)
1555	1477/76/78	49 Ráxasa	The Emperor Acbar succeeded Humayoon.
1556	1478/79/81	50 Nala	
1557	1479/78/80/90	51 Pingala	S. Ranga RD. ruled Penugonda.
1558	1480/79/81	52 Kálayucti	Sadā Siva still ruled Vijayanagar (Beejnugger.)
1559	1481/82/86	53 Siddhárthi	Tirumala R. ruled Ghutti (Gooty.)
1560	1482/81/83	54 Raudri	Hari Hara D.
1561	1483/1480	55 Durmati	See Ferishta 3. 241—242. The Musulmans were forced to entreat Rāma Raya, and sue for peace.
1562	1484/83/89	56 Dundubhi	

A. D.	Sálivahana Sacam.	TITLE.	NOTES.
Probable.	True. *Variation.*		
1563	1485/1486	57 Rudiródgári	AH. 971. The Musulmans invaded Adhwani (Adhoni) they slew Aliya Rama R. —— Seif Khan became ruler of the Telugu country: and was expelled by Ibrahim Kutb Shah. Bri. Fer. III. 105, 235, 286, 384, 394. This is explained in page 110. Seif-ein-ul mulk was the rebellious servant of Ibrahim Adil Shah of Beejapoor and was slain. It appears Rama Raja and his younger brother Vencatadri Nayak, chiefs of Beejnugur aided Ibrahim Adil Shah. p. 105, 110, 235 [This Ramraz appears to be Aliya Rama Reddi son-in-law to Krishna Rayalu.] From the details given in p. 121,-123 and 241, 244 it is clear that he greatly humbled the Turk invaders: who at length formed a general league against him, p 124, p 246 which came to an issue in A. D. 1564 when they slew him.] In p. 126 Ferishta says that Aliya Rama Reddis second brother was Vencatadri [Nayuda] and the youngest brother was 'Yeltumray' [that is, Aliya Timma Ra[illegible]] "Narapati" of Anegondi; the battle happened on 26th December, 1564 at Raxasa Tangadi on the banks of the river Krishna. The Turks then plundered Vijayanagar. Ferishta, p. 126 gives long details, he says that Aliya Rama Raz was seventy years of age. The Hindu MSS. omit all particulars of this final ruin of Vijayanagar.
1564	1486	58 Ractáxi	Hari Hara R.. Achyuta R. Ananta R. Narasa RDMR.
1565	1487/1486	59 Kródhana	
1566	1488/1490	60 Xaya	Termination of the rule of the Vaddeh barons, in most towns.
1567	1489/86/88	1 Prabhava	Cycle LXXVIII.
1568	1490	2 Vibhava	The '*Turks*' conquered 'Kadapa' (Cuddapa.) Ferishta's history states that in these wars the Musulman troops were chiefly *Turks* and led by *Turkish* commanders. Hence among Hindus in southern India the name *Turk* is wrongly used instead of Musulman to this day.
1569	1491	3 S'ucla	Narasinga R. ruled Vijayanagar and now conquered Penagonda.
1570	1492	4 Pramódúta	A Solar eclipse. The vasu Charitra was written. Death of Sadā Siva who ruled 23 years.
1571	1493/92/94	5 Prajótpatti	
1572	1494/1495	6 A'ngi'rasa	S. Ranga DMR. Death of Abdul Nabi Khan. Anā Véma Reddi ruled Rajamahendri until this year, when the Turks took it.
1573	1495	7 Srímukha	Vencatesa R. is conquered by Ali Adel Shah. (Ferishta.)
1574	1496/1497	8 Bháva	
1575	1497/1498	9 Yuva	End of reign of Achyuta Rayalu.
1576	1498/1499	10 Dhátu	
1577	1499	11 I's'wara	VPS. Ranga DMR. ruled Penagonda.
1578	1500/1501	12 Bahudhánya	A lunar eclipse.
1579	1501	13 Pramádi	Kali 4680. Hejri 987.
1580	1502	14 Vicrama	Malik Ibrahim, king of the Karnatic conquered Kondavīdu.
1581	1503	15 Vishu	Pemmasāni Immadi Timma Nayu.
1582	1504/1505	16 Chitrabhánu	The petty barons of Kadapa rebel against the 'Turks.'
1583	1505/04/06	17 Swabhánu	Sancara Narayana Swami a celebrated saint.
1584	1506/1507	18 Tárana	
1585	1507/1506	19 Pārthiva	S. Ranga R. is succeeded by SV. Vencatapati RDMR. at Penagonda. Death of Pemmasāni Timma Nayu.
1586	1508/07/10	20 Vyaya	
1587	1509	21 Sarvajit	Queen Immadi Chenna Bhairava.
1588	1510	22 Sarvadhári	Nek nām Agha Mohammad was appointed by Alamgīr to rule Kaddapa.
1589	1511/10/12	23 Viródhi	
1590	1512/1511	24 Vicriti	

A. D.	Sáliváhana Sacam.	Title.	Hejri.	Notes.
Probable.	True. *Variation.*			
1591	1513/1515	25 Khara	1000	
1592	1514/15/16/24	26 Nandana	1001	Ghaṭṭ Endra Odayar: also called Ghanta Odayar.
1593	1515/12/16	27 Vijaya	1002	
1594	1516	28 Jaya	1003	Emperor Alamgīr sent Mir Jumla Zulfaccar Khan who conquered Pemmasani Reddi and took Gandícota.
1595	1517/1518	29 Manmatha	1004	V. Vencatapati D. Kali 4696. Collam (*i. e.* Quilon) 771.
1596	1518	30 Durmukhi	1005	
1597	1519/20/21/22	31 Hévilambi	1006	Haudeh Hanimi Náyar.
1598	1520	32 Vilambi	1007	Queen Chenna Bhairava Devi Ranga R. ruled Penagonda.
1599	1521/1522	33 Vicári	1008	Sadā Siva, son of Achyuta D...Malik Ibrahim.
1600	1522	34 Sārvari	1009	Maṭla Anantaiia D. Choda R. son of Ellam Raz.
1601	1523/1524	35 Plava	1010	V. Vencatapati RD ruled Nidigallu, Vencatagiri and Penagonda.
1602	1524/1525	36 Subhacrit	1011	
1603	1525	37 Sóbhacrit	1012	Sōḍeh Arasapa Nayacar.
1604	1526/1522	38 Kródhi	1013	Mohammad Kūlī Khan.
1605	1527/28/29	39 Visvāvas	1014	Acbar dies and is succeeded by Jehangīr.
1606	1528/21/29	40 Parábhava	1015	Gobbūri Giriappa ruled Srī Sailam.
1607	1529/1530	41 Plavanga	1016	Insurrection in Hydrabad (Ferishta 3. 476.)
1608	1530/1531	42 Kílaca	1017	Duhoor near Cuddapa was seized by the 'Turks.'
1609	1531/1532	43 Saumya	1018	
1610	1532/1533	44 Sádháraná	1019	Abdul Mohammed Khan appointed Jillēlla Rangapati who commanded Gandicota SS. 1508—1532.
1611	1533/1532	45 Viródhicrit	1020	Kali 4722. Vicramad 1668. Collam 787.
1612	1534/33/38	46 Parídhávi	1021	The English traders first landed at Surat.
1613	1535	47 Pramādícha	1022	SV Vencatapati DMR ruled Dúpād and Penugonda.
1614	1536	48 A'nanda	1023	Sultan Abd-ul-Kutb Shah.
1615	1537	49 Ráxasa	1024	Sir Thos. Roe reached Agra as an Ambassador from King James I.
1616	1538/1539	50 Nala	1025	
1617	1539	51 Pingala	1026/7	
1618	1540/1541	52 Kālayucti	1028	S. Bhairava Bhúpati.
1619	1541/42/46	53 Siddhārthi	1029	The 'Turks' conquered Kandanúl. (Curnool.)
1620	1542	54 Raudri	1030	
1621	1543/1545	55 Durmati	1031	Pemmasani Timma Nayudu.
1622	1544	56 Dundubhi	1032	Malli RDR.
1623	1545	57 Rudiródgāri	1033	Achyuta Rāma Kaunden.
1624	1546	58 Ractāxi	1034	SVPSV Rama DMR ruled Penagonda.
1625	1547	59 Kródhana	1035	
1626	1548/1549	60 Xaya	1036	The English began to trade at Pulicat.
1627	1549/1550	1 Prabhava	1037	Kali 4728. Vicr. 1684. First year of Cycle 79. Vencatappa Nayudu.
1628	1550/49/53	2 Vibhava	1038	Jehāngi'r, Emperor of Delhi is succeeded by Shah Jehan.
1629	1551/1550	3 S'ucla	1039	Collam Æra 804.
1630	1552/1553	4 Pramódúta	1040	Rama R. or Rama DR. Fra Paolino de San Bartolomeo asserts that in A. D. 1630 Pudicheri (Pondicherry) was given up to the French by Sivaji the Marata chief. But Sivaji was at this date only four years old.

A. D.	Sálivâhana Sacam.	Title.	Hejri.	Fasly.	Notes.
Proba-ble.	True. *Variation.*				
1631	1553/1554	5 Prajótpatti	1041	1040	
1632	1554	6 A'ngi'rasa	1042	1041	
1633	1555/1556	7 Srímukha	1043	1042	Kempana Vadeyar.
1634	1556/55/57				V. Vencatapati RDMR. ruled Penagonda.
		8 Bhâva	1044	1043	The English traders were first permitted to enter the Ganges.
1635	1557				
1636	1558	9 Yuva	1045	1044	
1637	1559	10 Dhátu	1046	1045	
1638	1560/1561	11 I's'wara	1047	1046	Keladi V. Bhadrappa Nâyacar.
		12 Bahudhânya	1048	1047	Kanṭhírava Narasa Vadeyar This name Kanṭhírava (meaning Lion) has been changed into Cantaroy. Hence the "Cantaroy fanam."
1639	1561	13 Pramádi	1049	1048	Vencatabati D. . Krishna DMR.
					V. Bhadrapa . . Handeh Siddha Ramapi.
1640	1562/1563	14 Vicrama	1050	1049	The English first settled at Madras and named it Fort St. George, which was subordinate to Bantam. (Bintang.)
1641	1563/1562	15 Vishu	1051	1050	Narasa R. Vadeyar ruled Mysore.
1642	1564/1563	16 Chitrabhánu	1052	1051	
1643	1565	17 Swabhánu	1053	1052	Shyâma R. Vadeyar.
					Krishna R. Vadeyar.
1644	1566	18 Tárana	1054	1053	Kali 4745 Vicram. 1701 . . Pemmasâni Timma Nayudu ruled Gandicota (hitherto ruled by Timma Raz for 33 years.)
1645	1567/66/70	19 Pārthiva	1055	1054	The Turks conquered Cuddapa.
1646	1568	20 Vyaya	1056	1055	
1647	1569/1571	21 Sarvajit	1057	1056	Chikka DR. Vadeyar.
					R. Vizaia Ranga Socca Natha Nayudu of (Trisiram) Trichinopoly was succeeded by Bangaru Tirumala Nayudu.
1648	1570	22 Sarvadhári	1058	1057	Handeh Malacapa Nayudu ruled Bellary. . . . SVPSV Ranga RDMR. ruled Penagonda.
1649	1571	23 Viródhi	1059	1058	Mohammad Shah Padshah.
1650	1572/1571	24 Vicriti	1060 1061	1059	
1651	1573	25 Khara	1062	1060	
1652	1574	26 Nandana	1063	1061	
1653	1575	27 Vijaya	1064	1062	Fort St. George becomes a Presidency with two factors and ten soldiers.
					Abdul Kutub Shah.
					Sayad Mir Husén (alias Nek-nam-Khan-Bahadar.)
1654	1576/1575	28 Jaya	1065	1063	
1655	1577/78/79	29 Manmatha	1066	1064	Keladi Soma Sekhara Nayac.
1656	1578	30 Durmukhi	1067	1065	Sultan Muhammad Adil Padshah.
1657	1579/1562	31 Hévilambi	1068	1066	S. Ranga DMR.
1658	1580	32 Vilambi	1069	1067	Bhāganagar near Golconda becomes a city ; now called Hyderabad.
1659	1581/82/87/91	33 Vicári	1070	1068	The English trade begins to thrive. From SS. 1568 till 1582 Gandicota was ruled by Ahmad Begh.
1660	1582/1583	34 Sárvari	1071	1069	
1661	1583/1582	35 Plava	1072	1070	Kali 4762. Vicram. 1718 Bhadrapa Nayac.

A. D.	Sáliváhana Sacam.	Title.	Hejri.	Fasly.	Notes.
	True. *Variation.*				
1662	1584/1585	36 Subhacrit	1073	1071	Khoja Daood Khan ruled Kudapa being sent from Delhi by the Emperor. He appointed Abdul Nabi Khan ruler of Kadapa. Deva R. Wadeyar ruled Mysore. Keladi Soma Sekhara Nayac.
1663	1585/80/86/90	37 Sóbhacrit	1074	1072	The Vijayanagar dynasty ends with S. Ranga R.
1664	1586	38 Kródhi	1075	1073	Chikka DR. Wadeyar. Sivaji the Mahratta plundered Sura- and Kurnool.
1665	1587/88/92	39 Visvāvas	1076	1074	Abdul Hasn, Kutbul Mulk (called Tannashah) ruled Golconda.
1666	1588	40 Parābhava	1077	1075	
1667	1589/86/90	41 Plavanga	1078	1076	
1668	1590	42 Kílaca	1079	1077	Sōdē Savāi Rama Chandra Nayacar Mumbaee *i. e.* Bombay was ceded to the East India Company.
1669	1591	43 Saumya	1080	1078	Kollam year 844.
1670	1592/1594	44 Sādhāraná	1081	1079	
1671	1593/1594	45 Viródhicrit	1082	1080	
1672	1594/1595	46 Parídhāvi	1083	1081	A great battle at Tanjore.
1673	1595/96/97	47 Pramādícha	1084	1082	Banavasi in Soonda was ruled by Sōdē Savāyi Rama Chandra Nayac.
1674	1596/95/97	48 A′nanda	1085	1083	
1675	1597	49 Rāxasa	1086	1084	
1676	1598/1597	50 Nala	1087	1085	Penagonda was ruled by Vencatapati Nayac.
1677	1599	51 Pingala	1088	1086	Vencata DMR ruled Trichinopoly.
1678	1600/1596	52 Kālayucti	1089	1087	Kali 4779. Vicram 1735. Chikka DR. Vadeyar. Matla Vencat Rama R. Choda MR.
1679	1601	53 Siddhārthi	1090	1088	
1680	1602	54 Raudri	1091	1089	Keladi Chennama Jiyar, a Baroness.
1681	1603	55 Durmati	1092	1090	Death of Sivaji, founder of the Mahratta Empire.
1682	1604	56 Dundubhi	1093/4	1091/2	
1683	1605/1606	57 Rudiródgári	1095	1092	Termination of the kingdom of (Vizayāpuram) Beejapoor.
1684	1606/05/11	58 Ractāxi	1096	1093	
1685	1607/06/08	59 Kródhana	1097	1094	
1686	1608/1609	60 Xaya	1098	1095	A famine.
1687	1609/1610	1 Prabhava	1099	1096	Cycle LXXX. begins. Aurungzebe conquered Golconda. Bhāganagar (since called Hydrabad) was ruled by Sikander Ghāzi ud Dín.
1688	1610/1609	2 Vibhava	1100	1097	
1689	1611/03/09/12	3 S′ucla	1101	1098	Matla Vencata Rama DR Chola MR.
1690	1612	4 Pramódúta	1102	1099	
1691	1613	5 Prajótpatti	1103	1100	The Condavíd country was ruled by Mubārik Khan as Subedar of the Deccan.
1692	1614/1615	6 A′ngi′rasa	1104	1101	The English purchased Cuddalore from Rāma Rāja.
1693	1615/1614	7 Srímukha	1105	1102	A new Charter was granted to the East India Company.
1694	1616/1615	8 Bhāva	1106	1103	Kali 4795. Vicrama 1751.

A. D.	Sálivábana Sacâm.	Title.	Hejri.	Fasly.	Notes.
	True. *Variation.*				
1695	1617/1618	9 Yuva	1107	1104	Zanzí (Gingee) was taken by the Moguls from the Mahrattas.
1696	1618/17/19/21	10 Dhátu	1108	1105	Matla Kumāra Yācham Nāyudu.
1697	1619/1620	11 I's'wara	1109	1106	Daood Khan was slain. He had ruled Kuddapa from A. D. 1661 until 1696.
1698	1620	12 Bahudhānya	1110	1107	A new E. I. Company was established.
1699	1621/1622	13 Pramádi	1111	1108	Keladi Basavapa Nāyac. Matla Ananta Rama.
1700	1622/1623	14 Vicrama	1112	1109	The rivalry of the old and new E. I. Companies ruined all trade. The native rulers took bribes from both parties.
1701	1623/1624	15 Vishu	1113	1110	
1702	1624/26/29	16 Chitrabhánu	1114	1111	Fazil Ali Khan, alias Gul-Khan.
1703	1625	17 Swabhánu	1115	1112	Sadā Siva Raya. Kumāra Ananta Rama RD. Chola MR.
1704	1626	18 Tárana	1116	1113	Murāri Rao of Gooty invaded Kaddapa.
1705	1627	19 Pārthiva	1117	1114	Kanthī-rava-Narasa R. Wadeyar.
1706	1628/1626	20 Vyaya	1118	1115	Kumāra Yacham Nayudu of Vencatagiri.
1707	1629/21/28	21 Sarvajit	1119	1116	Death of Aurungzebe. At Madras there were 300 Europeans; of whom 200 were military.
1708	1630/29/31	22 Sarvadhári	1120	1117	The E. I. Company was established.
1709	1631/29/32	23 Viródhi	1121	1118	
1710	1632/1633	24 Vicriti	1122	1119	Asaf Jah Nizam ul Mulk ruled Golconda. Saadat Ali Khan of Arcot ruled the Carnatic.
1711	1633/1635	25 Khara	1123	1120	Abdul Nabi Khan Mayana ruled Gandicota. He sent Fatteh Sing to rule (Siddha-vatam) Siddhout.
1712	1634/36/37	26 Nandana	1124	1121	
1713	1635/1637	27 Vijaya	1125	1122	Kali 4814. Vicramdit 1770. Vijayanagar was ruled by A'nanda Rao.
1714	1636/1637	28 Jaya	1126	1123	
1715	1637	29 Manmatha	1127/8	1124	
1716	1638/1637	30 Durmukhi	1129	1125	
1717	1639/1638	31 Hévilambi	1130	1126	Battle at Siddhaut between Mayāna Abdul Nabi Khan and Fatih Sing servant of Saadat Ulla Khan of Arcot. Abdul Nabi's son was Abdul Hamīd Khan, alias Hammū Miyan: alias Bara Miyān; who ruled Siddhavat from SS. 1639 until SS. 1666.
1718	1640	32 Vilambi	1131	1127	Abdul Husen Khan. Khoja Ahmad.
1719	1641/39/42	33 Vicári	1132	1128	
1720	1642/1641	34 Sárvari	1133	1129	
1721	1643	35 Plava	1134	1130	Matla Kumara Ananta R. ruled Penagonda.

A. D.	Sálivāhana Sacam.	Title.	Hejri.	Fasly.	Notes.
	True. *Variation.*			True. *Variation.*	
1722	1644/43/46	36 Subhacrit	1135	1131/32	A Frenchman named Mons. Quelasqui ? ruled Rēpallēh.
1723	1645/1646	37 Sóbhacrit	1136	1132	
1724	1646	38 Królhi	1137	1133/29	The French capture Mahé. Battle of Kamman Halli. (Or, otherwise, Gōman palli ?)
1725	1647	39 Visvávas	1138	1134	
1726	1648	40 Parábhava	1139	1135/31	Mayāna Abdul Nabi Khañ ruled Kadapa. The Court of Mayor and Alderman was established at Madras.
1727	1649/1650	41 Plavanga	1140	1136	
1728	1650	42 Kílaca	1141	1137	The Nabob of Kadapa bestowed Gandicota on Chemmu Miyān.
1729	1651/49/50	43 Saumya	1142	1138	Kali 4830. Vicrama 1788. Collam 905.
1730	1652/1653	44 Sádháraná	1143	1139/35	Abdul Nabi Khan of Kadapa: his son Nawab Hamīd Khan was succeeded by his brother Abdul Mosim Khan: alias Mō chā Mīyān.
1731	1653/1654	45 Viródhicrit	1144	1140/36	
1732	1654/53/55	46 Parídhāvi	1145	1141	
1733	1655/1656	47 Pramádícha	1146	1142/43	Bangāru Tirumala Nayudu.
1734	1656/1655	48 A'nanda	1147	1143	
1735	1657/1658	49 Ráxasa	1148	1144	
1736	1658/56/59	50 Nala	1149	1145	
1737	1659/1660	51 Pingala	1150	1146	
1738	1660/1658	52 Kālayucti	1151	1147	
1739	1661	53 Siddhárthi	1152	1148/50	Kollam year 915.
1740	1662/1663	54 Raudri	1153	1149	Kadapa was plundered by the Mahrattas.
1741	1663/1665	55 Durmati	1154	1150	Mons. Dupleix became governor of Pondicherry.
1742	1664/1663	56 Dundubhi	1155	1151	The English took Trichinopoly: and again lost it to Nizam ul-Mulk.
1743	1665	57 Rudiródgāri	1156	1152	
1744	1666/1667	58 Ractáxi	1157	1153/54	War commences between the French and English.
1745	1667/1666	59 Krodhana	1158	1154	
1746	1668	60 Xaya	1159	1155	
1747	1669/1668	1 Prabhava	1160	1156/55	Kali 4848 Vicramad 1804. Beginning of Cycle LXXXI. Hyder's first victory at Balāpur. Death of Abdul Nabi Khan Mayana who ruled Kadapa from SS. 1658 until 1669. Alaf Khan dies: and is succeeded by his brother Ranad Ullā Khan. He after a reign of one year was succeeded by Alaf Khan's son Himmat Bahádar: who reigned twenty years.
1748	1670	2 Vibhava	1161/2	1157/58	Death of Nizam Asaf Jah.
1749	1671/1670	3 S'ucla	1163	1158/60	Battle of A'mūr, or ābōōr-ghur: on 2d Dec. (*Ambour.*)
1750	1672/1673	4 Pramódúta	1164	1159	Nasir Jung was slain, 5th Dec.
1751	1673/1671	5 Prajótpatti	1165	1160	Clive took Arcot.

A. D.	Sálivâhana Sacam.	Title.	Hejri.	Fasly.	Notes.
	True. *Variation.*			True. *Variation.*	
1752	1674/1673	6 A'ngi'rasa	1166	1161/62	Birth of Tippu Sultan.
1753	1675/76/79	7 Srímukha	1167	1162/63	Hyder besieged Trichinopoly.
1754	1676	8 Bháva	1168	1163	Death of Himmat Bahader. The French held Masulipatam and Ganjam.
1755	1677/1678	9 Yuva	1169	1164	
1756	1678/75/80	10 Dhátu	1170	1165	Hyder conquered Seringapatam.
1757	1679/1680	11 I's'wara	1171	1166	Battle of (Palásí) Plassey 23d June.
1758	1680/79/85	12 Bahudhánya	1172	1167	Mons Lally attacked Tanjore and Madras.
1759	1681/1680	13 Pramádi	1173	1168	The French raised the siege of Madras.
1760	1682/1686	14 Vicrama	1174	1169	(January) The English expelled the French from (Vandēvāsī) Wandewash.
1761	1683/1684	15 Vishu	1175	1170/71	Hyder vanquished Khandeh Rao. Battle of Panipat. 7th Jan. 1761.
1762	1684/1687	16 Chitrabhánu	1176	1171/72	Kali 4863. Vicramad 1819.
1763	1685/1686	17 Swabhánu	1177	1172	
1764	1686/1687	18 Tārana	1178	1173	
1765	1687	19 Pārthiva	1179	1174	
1766	1688/1687	20 Vyaya	1180	1175	Nizam Ali leagues with the English and also with Hyder. The English took Rajahmandry.
1767	1689/1690	21 Sarvajit	1181	1176	War began between Hyder and the English. Battle of Errodu.
1768	1690	22 Sarvadhári	1182	1177	Hyder attacked Madras. Battle at Malvāgal, or Manbāgal on 4th October 1768.
1769	1691/1692	23 Viródhi	1183	1178	Hyder forced the English to make peace.
1770	1692/1691	24 Vicriti	1184	1179	Nabob of Arcot invaded Tanjore.
1771	1693/1694	25 Khara	1185	1180/81	Gandicota was four times plundered in fourteen years.
1772	1694/1695	26 Nandana	1186	1181	Lally governed Pondicheri. Pigott governed Madras.
1773	1695	27 Vijaya	1187	1182	I'gela Shyām Rao the Marata plundered Kaddapa and Tanjore.
1774	1696/95/97	28 Jaya	1188	1183	
1775	1697/96/99	29 Manmatha	1189	1184/83/85	The Maratas invade Kadapa.
1776	1698/1699	30 Durmukhi	1190	1185	
1777	1699/1700	31 Hévilambi	1191	1186	
1778	1700	32 Vilambi	1192	1187	The English took Pondicheri. Hyder vanquished the Nabob (Mayána) of Cuddapa.
1779	1701	33 Vicári	1193	1188/89	Kali 4880.
1780	1702/01/04	34 Sárvari	1194	1189	Hyder began his final plundering excursion.
1781	1703/1704	35 Plava	1195/6	1190	Sir Eyre Coote defeated Hyder near Porto Novo.
1782	1704/1702	36 Subhacrit	1197	1191	Death of Hyder; 6th Dec. 1782, the first day of Hejri 1197. Accession of Tippoo Sultan.
1783	1705/1706	37 Sóbhacrit	1198	1192	Guntoor (Mustafanagar) was ceded to the English.
1784	1706/1710	38 Kródhi	1199	1193	Bussy became Governor of Pondicheri.

A. D.	Sálivâhana Sacam.	Title.	Hejri.	Fasly.	Notes.
	True. *Variation.*			True. *Variation.*	
1785	1707/06/09/11	39 Visvávas	1200	1194/95/96	Gootty was plundered by the Marattas.
1786	1708/06/09	40 Parábhava	1201	1195/94/96	The English took Cuddalore.
1787	1709/1708	41 Plavanga	1202	1196/94/97	Tippoo attacked Adhoni.
1788	1710/1709	42 Kílaca	1203	1197	
1789	1711/1710	43 Saumya	1204	1198/96/99	Tippoo began to make war on the English.
1790	1712/1711	44 Sādháraná	1205	1199/98	The Nizam conquered Kadapa. The English took Bangalore.
1791	1713/1714	45 Viródhicrit	1206	1200/1199	Battle of Seringapatam. Cornwallis took Tippoo's camp.
1792	1714/1713	46 Parídhávi	1207	1201	The Marattas attack Bednore. A great famine, called Mina Sani Caruvu.
1793	1715/1714	47 Pramādícha	1208	1202	The English took Pondicherry.
1794	1716/15/17	48 A'nanda	1209	1203	
1795	1717/1716	49 Ráxasa	1210	1204	Year 971 of the Quilon (Collam) or Parasurāma Æra.
1796	1718	50 Nala	1211	1205	
1797	1719/1718	51 Pingala	1212	1206	
1798	1720/1718	52 Kálayucti	1213	1207	Tippoo invaded Coorg.
1799	1721/20	53 Siddhárthi	1214	1208	Fall of Seringapatam. Death of Tippoo Sultan.
1800	1722/1721	54 Raudri	1215	1209	The Company's government of Cuddapa and Bellary began.
1801	1723/1722	55 Durmati	1216	1210	
1802	1724/1723	56 Dundubhi	1217	1211	
1803	1725	57 Rudiródgári	1218	1212	
1804	1726	58 Ractáxi	1219	1213/14	A storm and flood for three days at Cuddapa.
1805	1727/1724	59 Kródhana	1220	1214	
1806	1728/1726	60 Xaya	1221	1215	A famine in Cuddapa.
1807	1729	1 Prabhava	1222	1216	Beginning of Cycle LXXXII.
1808	1730/1729	2 Vibhava	1223	1217	
1809	1731	3 S'ucla	1224	1218	Kali 4910.
1810	1732	4 Pramódúta	1225	1219	
1811	1733/1732	5 Prajótpatti	1226	1220	
1812	1734	6 A'ngi'rasa	1227	1221	
1813	1735/1736	7 Srímukha	1228/9	1222	
1814	1736	8 Bhāva	1230	1223	
1815	1737	9 Yuva	1231	1224	
1816	1738	10 Dhātu	1232	1225	
1817	1739	11 I's'wara	1233	1226	
1818	1740	12 Bahudhánya	1234	1227	
1819	1741	13 Pramádi	1235	1228	
1820	1742	14 Vicrama	1236	1229	
1821	1743	15 Vishu	1237	1230	
1822	1744	16 Chitrabhánu	1238	1231	
1823	1745	17 Swabhanu	1239	1232	
1824	1746	18 Tārana	1240	1233	
1825	1747	19 Pārthiva	1241	1234	
1826	1748	20 Vyaya	1242	1235	
1827	1749	21 Sarvajit	1243	1236	
1828	1750	22 Sarvadhāri	1244	1237	
1829	1751	23 Viródhi	1245	1238	

A. D.	Sálivâhana Sacam.	Title.	Hejri.	Fasly.	Notes.
1830	1752	24 Vicriti	1246	1239	
1831	1753	25 Khara	1247	1240	
1832	1754	26 Nandana	1248	1241	
1833	1755	27 Vijaya	1249	1242	
1834	1756	28 Jaya	1250	1243	
1835	1757	29 Manmatha	1251	1244	
1836	1758	30 Durmukhi	1252	1245	
1837	1759	31 Hévilambi	1253	1246	
1838	1760	32 Vilambi	1254	1247	
1839	1761	33 Vicári	1255	1248	
1840	1762	34 Sárvari	1256	1249	
1841	1763	35 Plava	1257	1250	
1842	1764	36 Subhacrit	1258	1251	
1843	1765	37 Sóbhacrit	1259	1252	Annexation of Saindhava (Scinde) : in the Mahomedan year 1260.
1844	1766	38 Kródhi	1260	1253	
1845	1767	39 Visvávas	1261/2	1254	
1846	1768	40 Parábhava	1263	1255	
1847	1769	41 Plavanga	1264	1256	
1848	1770	42 Kílaca	1265	1257	
1849	1771	43 Saumya	1266	1258	
1850	1772	44 Sádháraná	1267	1259	
1851	1773	45 Viródhicrit	1268	1260	
1852	1774	46 Parídhávi	1269	1261	
1853	1775	47 Pramádícha	1270	1262	
1854	1776	48 A'nanda	1271	1263	
1855	1777	49 Ráxasa	1272	1264	
1856	1778	50 Nala	1273	1265	
1857	1779	51 Pingala	1274	1266	
1858	1780	52 Kálayucti	1275	1267	
1859	1781	53 Siddhárthi	1276	1268	
1860	1782	54 Raudri	1277	1269	
1861	1783	55 Durmati	1278	1270	
1862	1784	56 Dundubhi	1279	1271	
1863	1785	57 Rudiródgári	1280	1272	
1864	1786	58 Ractáxi	1281	1273	
1865	1787	59 Kródhana	1282	1274	
1866	1788	60 Xaya	1283	1275	

SYNONYMOUS KEY.

In the following two tables any Cyclic year in the last three centuries (between the 77th and 82d cycles,) may be easily found.

In the first table the sixty names stand in the Indian Cyclic order. In the second they are arranged according to the English alphabet.

Thus if we meet with a document dated in the year Pārthiva: the first table shews that year to fall in the Indian years 1747, 1687, 1627, 1567, 1507, 1447 : and the second table shews that these answer respectively to years 1825, 1765, 1705, 1645, 1585 and 1525, of the English Chronology. For the same name recurs after every sixty years.

And Parthiva, in the Alphabetical list is marked 19: this shews that it is the nineteenth year in the other list.

C. P. BROWN.

MADRAS,
November, 1849.

(First Table.) YEARS OF THE SALIVAHANA SACAM.

Cycle SAL. SAC.	77th	78th	79th	80th	81st	82nd.
Prabhava, 1	1429	1489	1549	1609	1669	1729
Vibhava, 2	1430	1490	1550	1610	1670	1730
S'ucla, 3	1431	1491	1551	1611	1671	1731
Pramódúta, 4	1432	1492	1552	1612	1672	1732
Prajótpatti, 5	1433	1493	1553	1613	1673	1733
A'ngi'rasa, 6	1434	1494	1554	1614	1674	1734
Srímukha, 7	1435	1495	1555	1615	1675	1735
Bháva, 8	1436	1496	1556	1616	1676	1736
Yuva, 9	1437	1497	1557	1617	1677	1737
Dhátu, 10	1438	1498	1558	1618	1678	1738
I's'wara, 11	1439	1499	1559	1619	1679	1739
Bahudhánya, 12	1440	1500	1560	1620	1680	1740
Pramádi, 13	1441	1501	1561	1621	1681	1741
Vicrama, 14	1442	1502	1562	1622	1682	1742
Vishu, 15	1443	1503	1563	1623	1683	1743
Chitrabhánu, 16	1444	1504	1564	1624	1684	1744
Swabhánu, 17	1445	1505	1565	1625	1685	1745
Tárana, 18	1446	1506	1566	1626	1686	1746
Pārthiva, 19	1447	1507	1567	1627	1687	1747
Vyaya, 20	1448	1508	1568	1628	1688	1748
Sarvajit, 21	1449	1509	1569	1629	1689	1749
Sarvadhári, 22	1450	1510	1570	1630	1690	1750
Viródhi, 23	1451	1511	1571	1631	1691	1751
Vicriti, 24	1452	1512	1572	1632	1692	1752
Khara, 25	1453	1513	1573	1633	1693	1753
Nandana, 26	1454	1514	1574	1634	1694	1754
Vijaya, 27	1455	1515	1575	1635	1695	1755
Jaya, 28	1456	1516	1576	1636	1696	1756
Manmatha, 29	1457	1517	1577	1637	1697	1757
Durmukhi, 30	1458	1518	1578	1638	1698	1758
Hévilambi, 31	1459	1519	1579	1639	1699	1759
Vilambi, 32	1460	1520	1580	1640	1700	1760
Vicári, 33	1461	1521	1581	1641	1701	1761
Sárvari, 34	1462	1522	1582	1642	1702	1762
Plava, 35	1463	1523	1583	1643	1703	1763
Subhacrit, 36	1464	1524	1584	1644	1704	1764
Sóbhacrit, 37	1465	1525	1585	1645	1705	1765
Kródhi, 38	1466	1526	1586	1646	1706	1766
Visvávas, 39	1467	1527	1587	1647	1707	1767
Parábhava, 40	1468	1528	1588	1648	1708	1768
Plavanga, 41	1469	1529	1589	1649	1709	1769
Kílaca, 42	1470	1530	1590	1650	1710	1770
Saumya, 43	1471	1531	1591	1651	1711	1771
Sádháraná, 44	1472	1532	1592	1652	1712	1772
Viródhicrit, 45	1473	1533	1593	1653	1713	1773
Parídhávi, 46	1474	1534	1594	1654	1714	1774
Pramádícha, 47	1475	1535	1595	1655	1715	1775
A'nanda, 48	1476	1536	1596	1656	1716	1776
Ráxasa, 49	1477	1537	1597	1657	1717	1777
Nala, 50	1478	1538	1598	1658	1718	1778
Pingala, 51	1479	1539	1599	1659	1719	1779
Kálayucti, 52	1480	1540	1600	1660	1720	1780
Siddhárthi, 53	1481	1541	1601	1661	1721	1781
Raudri, 54	1482	1542	1602	1662	1722	1782
Durmati, 55	1483	1543	1603	1663	1723	1783
Dundubhi, 56	1484	1544	1604	1664	1724	1784
Rudiródgári, 57	1485	1545	1605	1665	1725	1785
Ractáxi, 58	1486	1546	1606	1666	1726	1786
Kródhana, 59	1487	1547	1607	1667	1727	1787
Xaya, 60	1488	1548	1608	1668	1728	1788

(Second Table.) ANSWERING TO THESE DATES A. D.

	ANN. DOM.					
A'nanda, 48	1494	1554	1614	1674	1734	1794
A'ngi'rasa, 6	1512	1572	1632	1692	1752	1812
Bahudhánya, 12	1518	1578	1638	1698	1758	1818
Bháva, 8	1514	1574	1634	1694	1754	1814
Chitrabhánu, 16	1522	1582	1642	1702	1762	1822
Dhátu, 10	1516	1576	1636	1696	1756	1816
Dundubhí, 56	1502	1562	1622	1682	1742	1802
Durmati, 55	1501	1561	1621	1681	1741	1801
Durmukhi, 30	1536	1596	1656	1716	1776	1836
Hévilambi, 31	1537	1597	1657	1717	1777	1837
I's'wara, 11	1517	1577	1637	1697	1757	1817
Jaya, 28	1534	1594	1654	1714	1774	1834
Kálayucti, 52	1498	1558	1618	1678	1738	1798
Khara, 25	1531	1591	1651	1711	1771	1831
Kílaca, 42	1488	1548	1608	1668	1728	1788
Kródhana, 59	1505	1565	1625	1685	1745	1805
Kródhi, 38	1544	1604	1664	1724	1784	844
Manmatha, 29	1535	1595	1655	1715	1775	1835
Nala, 50	1496	1556	1616	1676	1736	1796
Nandana, 26	1532	1592	1652	1712	1772	1832
Parábhava, 40	1546	1606	1666	1726	1786	1846
Parídhávi, 46	1492	1552	1612	1672	1732	1792
Párthiva, 19	1525	1585	1645	1705	1765	1825
Pingala, 51	1497	1557	1617	1677	1737	1797
Plava, 35	1541	1601	1661	1721	1781	1841
Plavanga, 41	1547	1607	1667	1727	1787	1847
Prabhava, 1	1507	1567	1627	1687	1747	1807
Prajótpatti, 5	1511	1571	1631	1691	1751	1811
Pramádi, 13	1519	1579	1639	1699	1759	1819
Pramádícha, 47	1493	1553	1613	1673	1733	1793
Pramódúta, 4	1510	1570	1630	1690	1750	1810
Ractáxi, 58	1504	1564	1624	1684	1744	1804
Raudri, 54	1500	1560	1620	1680	1740	1800
Ráxasa, 49	1495	1555	1615	1675	1735	1795
Rudiródgári, 57	1503	1563	1623	1683	1743	1803
Sádháraná, 44	1490	1550	1610	1670	1730	1790
Sarvadhári, 22	1528	1588	1648	1708	1768	1828
Sarvajit, 21	1527	1587	1647	1707	1767	1827
Sárvari, 34	1540	1600	1660	1720	1780	1840
Saumya, 43	1489	1549	1609	1669	1729	1789
Siddhárti, 53	1499	1559	1619	1679	1739	1799
Sóbhacrit, 37	1543	1603	1663	1723	1783	1843
Srímukha, 7	1513	1573	1633	1693	1753	1813
Subhacrit, 36	1542	1602	1662	1722	1782	1842
S'ucla, 3	1509	1569	1629	1689	1749	1809
Swabhánu, 17	1523	1583	1643	1703	1763	1823
Tárana, 18	1524	1584	1644	1704	1764	1824
Vibhava, 2	1508	1568	1628	1688	1748	1808
Vicári, 33	1539	1599	1659	1719	1779	1839
Vicrama, 14	1520	1580	1640	1700	1760	1820
Vicriti, 24	1530	1590	1650	1710	1770	1830
Vijaya, 27	1533	1593	1653	1713	1773	1833
Vilambi, 32	1538	1598	1658	1718	1778	1838
Viródhi, 23	1529	1589	1649	1709	1769	1829
Viródhicrit, 45	1491	1551	1611	1671	1731	1791
Vishu, 15	1521	1581	1641	1701	1761	1821
Vis'vávas, 39	1545	1605	1665	1725	1785	1845
Vyaya, 20	1526	1586	1646	1706	1766	1826
Xaya, or Axaya, 60	1506	1566	1626	1686	1746	1806
Yuva, 9	1515	1575	1635	1695	1755	1815

INDEX OF DATES.

(ANNO DOMINI.)

REGARDING THE PRINCIPAL NAMES IN THESE TABLES.

TABLE OF KALI YEARS.

THE KALI ÆRA COMMENCES 3101 YEARS BEFORE CHRIST.

Titles.	KALI Years.	Before Christ.	Titles.	KALI Years.	Before Christ.
13 Pramádi			37 Sóbhacrit	24	
14 Vicrama	1	3100	38 Kródhi	25	
15 Vishu	2		39 Visvávas	26	
16 Chitrabhánu	3		40 Parábhava	27	
17 Swabhánu	4		41 Plavanga	28	
18 Tárana	5		42 Kílaca	29	
19 Pārthiva	6		43 Saumya	30	
20 Vyaya	7		44 Sádháraná	31	3070
21 Sarvajit	8		45 Viródhicrit	32	
22 Sarvadhári	9		46 Parídhávi	33	
23 Viródhi	10		47 Pramádícha	34	
24 Vicriti	11	3090	48 A'nanda	35	
25 Khara	12		49 Ráxasa	36	
26 Nandana	13		50 Nala	37	
27 Vijaya	14		51 Pingala	38	
28 Jaya	15		52 Kálayucti	39	
29 Manmatha	16		53 Siddhárthi	40	
30 Durmukhi	17		54 Raudri	41	3060
31 Hévilambi	18		55 Durmati	42	
32 Vilambi	19		56 Dundubhi	43	
33 Vicári	20		57 Rudiródgári	44	
34 Sárvari	21	3080	58 Ractáxi	45	
35 Plava	22		59 Kródhana	46	
36 Subhacrit	23		60 Xaya	47	3054

	Cycles,	1	2	3	4	5	6	7	8	9	10
1	Prabhava	48	108	168	228	288	348	408	468	528	588
2	Vibhava	B. C. 3053	2993	2933	2873	2813	2753	2693	2633	2573	2513
3	S'ucla										
4	Pramódúta										
5	Prajótpatti										
6	A'ngi'rasa										
7	Srímukha										
8	Bháva										
9	Yuva										
10	Dhátu										
11	I's'wara	58	118	178	238	298	358	418	478	538	598
12	Bahudhánya	B. C. 3043	2983	2923	2863	2803	2743	2683	2623	2563	2503
13	Pramádi										
14	Vicrama										
15	Vishu										
16	Chitrabhánu										
17	Swabhánu										
18	Tárana										
19	Pārthiva										
20	Vyaya										
21	Sarvajit	68	128	188	248	308	368	428	488	548	608
22	Sarvadhári	B. C 3033	2973	2913	2853	2793	2733	2673	2613	2553	2493
23	Viródhi										
24	Vicriti										
25	Khara										
26	Nandana										
27	Vijaya										
28	Jaya										
29	Manmatha										
30	Durmukhi										
31	Hévilambi	78	138	198	258	318	378	438	498	558	618
32	Vilambi	B. C. 3023	2963	2903	2843	2783	2723	2663	2603	2543	2483
33	Vicári										
34	S'árvari										
35	Plava										
36	S'ubhacrit										
37	S'óbhacrit										
38	Kródhi										
39	Vis'vávas										
40	Parábhava										
41	Plavanga	88	148	208	268	328	388	448	508	568	628
42	Kílaca	B. C. 3013	2953	2893	2833	2773	2713	2653	2593	2533	2473
43	Saumya										
44	Sádháraná										
45	Viródhicrit										
46	Parídhávi										
47	Pramádícha										
48	A'nanda										
49	Ráxasa										
50	Nala										
51	Pingala	98	158	218	278	338	398	458	518	578	638
52	Kálayucti	B. C. 3003	2943	2883	2823	2763	2703	2643	2583	2523	2463
53	Siddhárthi										
54	Raudri										
55	Durmati										
56	Dundubhi										
57	Rudiródgári										
58	Ractáxi										
59	Kródhana										
60	Xaya										

11	12	13	14	15	16	17	18	19	20	21	22
648	708	768	828	888	948	1008	1068	1128	1188	1248	1308
B. C. 2453	2393	2333	2273	2213	2153	2093	2033	1973	1913	1853	1793
658	718	778	838	898	958	1018	1078	1138	1198	1258	1318
B. C. 2443	2383	2323	2263	2203	2143	2083	2023	1963	1903	1843	1783
668	728	788	848	908	968	1028	1088	1148	1208	1268	1328
B. C. 2433	2373	2313	2253	2193	2133	2073	2013	1953	1893	1833	1773
678	738	798	858	918	978	1038	1098	1158	1218	1278	1338
B. C. 2423	2363	2303	2243	2183	2123	2063	2003	1943	1883	1823	1763
688	748	808	868	928	988	1048	1108	1166	1228	1288	1348
B. C. 2413	2353	2293	2233	2173	2113	2053	1993	1933	1873	1813	1753
698	758	818	878	938	998	1058	1118	1178	1238	1298	1358
B. C. 2403	2343	2283	2223	2163	2103	2043	1983	1923	1863	1803	1743

	Cycles, No.	23	24	25	26	27	28	29
1	Prabhava	1368	1428	1488	1548	1608	1668	1728
2	Vibhava							
3	S′ucla	B. C. 1733	1673	1613	1553	1493	1433	1373
4	Pramódúta							
5	Prajótpatti							
6	A′ngi′rasa							
7	Srímukha							
8	Bhāva							
9	Yuva							
10	Dhátu							
11	I′s′wara	1378	1438	1498	1558	1618	1678	1738
12	Bahudhánya							
13	Pramádi	B. C. 1723	1663	1603	1543	1483	1423	1363
14	Vicrama							
15	Vishu							
16	Chitrabhánu							
17	Swabhánu							
18	Tárana							
19	Pārthiva							
20	Vyaya							
21	Sarvajit	1388	1448	1508	1568	1628	1688	1748
22	Sarvadhári							
23	Viródhi	B. C. 1713	1653	1593	1533	1473	1413	1353
24	Vicriti							
25	Khara							
26	Nandana							
27	Vijaya							
28	Jaya							
29	Manmatha							
30	Durmukhi							
31	Hévilambi	1398	1458	1518	1578	1638	1698	1758
32	Vilambi							
33	Vicāri	B. C. 1703	1643	1583	1523	1463	1403	1343
34	S′ārvari							
35	Plava							
36	S′ubhacrit							
37	S′óbhacrit							
38	Kródhi							
39	Vis′vávas							
40	Parábhava							
41	Plavanga	1408	1468	1528	1588	1648	1708	1768
42	Kílaca							
43	Saumya	B. C. 1693	1633	1573	1513	1453	1393	1333
44	Sádháraná							
45	Viródhicrit							
46	Parídhávi							
47	Pramādícha							
48	A′nanda							
49	Rāxasa							
50	Nala							
51	Pingala	1418	1478	1538	1598	1658	1718	1778
52	Kálayucti							
53	Siddhárthi	B. C. 1683	1623	1563	1503	1443	1383	1323
54	Raudri							
55	Durmati							
56	Dundubhi							
57	Rudiródgāri							
58	Ractāxi							
59	Kródhaná							
60	Xaya							

30	31	32	33	34	35	36	37	38
1788	1848	1908	1968	2028	2088	2148	2208	2268
B. C. 1313	1253	1193	1133	1073	1013	953	893	833
1798	1858	1918	1978	2038	2098	2158	2218	2278
B. C. 1303	1243	1183	1123	1063	1003	943	883	823
1808	1868	1928	1988	2048	2108	2168	2228	2288
B. C. 1293	1233	1173	1113	1053	993	933	873	813
1818	1878	1938	1998	2058	2118	2178	2238	2298
B. C. 1283	1223	1163	1103	1043	983	923	863	803
1828	1888	1948	2008	2068	2128	2188	2248	2308
B. C. 1273	1213	1153	1093	1033	973	913	853	793
1838	1898	1958	2018	2078	2138	2198	2258	2318
B. C. 1263	1203	1143	1083	1023	963	903	843	783

	Cycles, No. 39	40	41	42	43
1 Prabhava	*Kali Æra.* 2328	2388	2448	2508	2568
2 Vibhava					
3 S′ucla	B. C. 773	713	653	593	533
4 Pramódúta					
5 Prajótpatti					
6 A′ngi′rasa					
7 Srímukha					
8 Bháva					
9 Yuva					
10 Dhátu					
11 I′s′wara....................	2338	2398	2458	2518	2578
12 Bahudhánya					
13 Pramádi	B. C. 763	703	643	583	523
14 Vicrama					
15 Vishu					
16 Chitrabhánu					
17 Swabhánu					
18 Tárana					
19 Pārthiva					
20 Vyaya					
21 Sarvajit....................	2348	2408	2468	2528	2588
22 Sarvadhári					
23 Viródhi	B. C. 753	693	633	573	513
24 Vicriti					
25 Khara					
26 Nandana					
27 Vijaya					
28 Jaya					
29 Manmatha					
30 Durmukhi					
31 Hévilambi....................	2358	2418	2478	2538	2598
32 Vilambi					
33 Vicāri	B. C. 743	683	623	563	503
34 S′ārvari					
35 Plava					
36 S′ubhacrit					
37 S′óbhacrit					
38 Kródhi					
39 Vis′vávas					
40 Parābhava					
41 Plavanga....................	2368	2428	2488	2548	2608
42 Kílaca					
43 Saumya	B. C. 733	673	613	553	493
44 Sādhárana					
45 Viródhicrit					
46 Parídhávi					
47 Pramádícha					
48 A′nanda					
49 Ráxasa					
50 Nala					
51 Pingala....................	2378	2438	2498	2558	2618
52 Kálayucti					
53 Siddhárthi	B. C. 723	663	603	543	483
54 Raudri					
55 Durmati					
56 Dundubhi					
57 Rudiródgári					
58 Ractáxi					
59 Kródhana					
60 Xaya					

44	45	46	47	48	49	50	51
2628	2688	2748	2808	2868	2928	2988	3048
B. C. 473	413	353	293	233	173	113	53
2638	2698	2758	2818	2878	2938	2998	3058
B. C. 463	403	343	283	223	163	103	43
2648	2708	2768	2828	2888	2948	3008	3068
B. C. 453	393	333	273	213	153	93	33
2658	2718	2778	2838	2898	2958	3018	3078
B. C. 443	383	323	263	203	143	83	23
2668	2728	2788	2848	2908	2968	3028	3088
B. C. 433	373	313	253	193	133	73	13
2678	2738	2798	2858	2918	2978	3038	3098
B. C. 423	363	303	243	183	123	63	3 B. C. 3101 A. D. 1 2 3 4 5 6

		Cycles, 52			53		
		Kali.		A. D.	K.	S. S.	A. D.
1	Prabhava	3108	——	7	3168		67
2	Vibhava						
3	S'ucla						
4	Pramódúta						
5	Prajótpatti						
6	A'ngi'rasa						
7	Srímukha						
8	Bháva						
9	Yuva						
10	Dhátu						
11	I's'wara	3118	——	17	3178		77
12	Bahudhánya				3179		
13	Pramádi				3180	1	First year
14	Vicrama				3181	2	of SS.
15	Vishu					3	
16	Chitrabhánu					4	
17	Swabhánu					5	
18	Tárana					6	
19	Pārthiva					7	
20	Vyaya					8	
21	Sarvajit	3128	——	27	3188	9	87
22	Sarvadhári					10	
23	Viródhi					11	
24	Vicriti					12	
25	Khara					13	
26	Nandana					14	
27	Vijaya					15	
28	Jaya					16	
29	Manmatha					17	
30	Durmukhi					18	
31	Hévilambi	3138	——	37	3198	19	97
32	Vilambi					20	
33	Vicári					21	
34	S'árvari					22	
35	Plava					23	
36	S'ubhacrit					24	
37	S'óbhacrit					25	
38	Haródhi					26	
39	Vis'vávas					27	
40	Parábhava					28	
41	Plavanga	3148	——	47	3208	29	107
42	Kílaca					30	
43	Saumya					31	
44	Sádháraná					32	
45	Viródhicrit					33	
46	Parídhávi					34	
47	Pramádícha					35	
48	A'nanda					36	
49	Ráxasa					37	
50	Nala					38	
51	Pingala	3158	——	57	3218	39	117
52	Kálayucti					40	
53	Siddhárthi					41	
54	Raudri					42	
55	Durmati					43	
56	Dundubhi					44	
57	Rudiródgári					45	
58	Ractáxi					46	
59	Iródhana					47	
60	Xaya					48	

54			55			56			57		
K	S.S.	A.D.	K.	S.S.	A.D.	K.	S.S.	A.D.	K.	S.S.	A.D.
3228	49	127	3288	109	187	3348	169	247	3408	229	307
3238	59	137	3298	119	197	3358	179	257	3418	239	317
3248	69	147	3308	129	207	3368	189	267	3428	249	327
3258	79	157	3318	139	217	3378	199	277	3438	259	337
3268	89	167	3328	149	227	3388	209	287	3448	269	347
3278	99	177	3338	159	237	3398	219	297	3458	279	357

Cycle of Brihaspati.	Cycle 58 K.	S.S.	A.D.	59 K.	S.S.	A.D.
1 Prabhava	3468	289	367	3528	349	427
2 Vibhava						
3 S′ucla						
4 Pramódúta						
5 Prajótpatti						
6 A′ngi′rasa						
7 Srímukha						
8 Bhāva						
9 Yuva						
10 Dhātu						
11 I′s′wara	3478	299	377	3538	359	437
12 Bahudhánya						
13 Pramādi						
14 Vicrama						
15 Vishu						
16 Chitrabhānu						
17 Swabhānu						
18 Tārana						
19 Pārthiva						
20 Vyaya						
21 Sarvajit	3488	309	387	3548	369	447
22 Sarvadhári						
23 Viródhi						
24 Vicriti						
25 Khara						
26 Nandana						
27 Vijaya						
28 Jaya						
29 Manmatha						
30 Durmukhi						
31 Hévilambi	3498	319	397	3558	379	457
32 Vilambi						
33 Vicári						
34 S′ārvari						
35 Plava						
36 S′ubhacrit						
37 S′óbhacrit						
38 Kródhi						
39 Vis′vávas						
40 Parábhava						
41 Plavanga	3508	329	407	3568	389	467
42 Kílaca						
43 Saumya						
44 Sādhāraná						
45 Viródhicrit						
46 Parídhāvi						
47 Pramādícha						
48 A′nanda						
49 Ráxasa						
50 Nala						
51 Pingala	3518	339	417	3578	399	477
52 Kálayucti						
53 Siddhárthi						
54 Raudri						
55 Durmáti						
56 Dundubhi						
57 Rudhiródgári						
58 Ractáxi						
59 Króilhana						
60 Xaya						

K.	60 S.S.	A.D	K.	61 S.S.	A.D.	K.	62 S.S.	A.D.
3588	409	487	3648	469	547	3708	529	607
3598	419	497	3658	479	557	3718	539	617
3608	429	507	3668	489	567	3728	549	627
3618	439	517	3678	499	577	3738	559	637
3628	449	527	3688	509	587	3748	569	647
3638	459	537	3698	519	597	3758	579	657

Cycle of Brihaspati.	Cycle 63 K.	S.S.	A.D.	64 K.	S.S.	A.D.
1 Prabhava	3768	589	667	3828	649	727
2 Vibhava						
3 S′ucla						
4 Pramódúta						
5 Prajótpatti						
6 A′ngi′rasa						
7 Srímukha						
8 Bháva						
9 Yuva						
10 Dhátu						
11 I′s′wara	3778	599	677	3838	659	737
12 Bahudhánya						
13 Pramádi						
14 Vicrama						
15 Vishu						
16 Chitrabhánu						
17 Swabhánu						
18 Tárana						
19 Párthiva						
20 Vyaya						
21 Sarvajit	3788	609	687	3848	669	747
22 Sarvadhári						
23 Viródhi						
24 Vicriti						
25 Khara						
26 Nandana						
27 Vijaya						
28 Jaya						
29 Manmatha						
30 Durmukhi						
31 Hévilambi	3798	619	697	3858	679	757
32 Vilambi						
33 Vicári						
34 S′árvari						
35 Plava						
36 S′ubhacrit						
37 S′óbhacrit						
38 Króbhi						
39 Vis′vávas						
40 Parábhava						
41 Plavanga	3808	629	707	3868	689	767
42 Kílaca						
43 Saumya						
44 Sádháraná						
45 Viródhicrit						
46 Parídhávi						
47 Pramádícha						
48 A′nanda						
49 Ráxasa						
50 Nala						
51 Pingala	3818	639	717	3878	699	777
52 Kálayucti						
53 Siddhárthi						
54 Raudri						
55 Durmati						
56 Dundubhi						
57 Rudhiródgári						
58 Ractáxi						
59 Kródhana						
60 Xaya						

K.	65 S.S.	A.D.	K.	66 S.S.	A.D.	K.	67 S.S.	A.D.	K.	68 S.S.	A.D.
3888	709	787	3948	769	847	4008	829	907	4068	889	967
3898	719	797	3958	779	857	4018	839	917	4078	899	977
3908	729	807	3968	789	867	4028	849	927	4088	909	987
3918	739	817	3978	799	877	4038	859	937	4098	919	997
3928	749	827	3988	809	887	4048	869	947	4108	929	1007
3938	759	837	3998	819	897	4058	879	957	4118	939	1017

Cycle of Brihaspati.	Cycle 69 K.	S.S.	A.D.	70 K.	S.S.	A.D.
1 Prabhava	4128	949	1027	4188	1009	1087
2 Vibhava						
3 S'ucla						
4 Pramódúta						
5 Prajótpatti						
6 A'ngi'rása						
7 Srímukha						
8 Bháva						
9 Yuva						
10 Dhátu						
11 I's'wara	4138	959	1037	4198	1019	1097
12 Bahudhánya						
13 Pramádi						
14 Vicrama						
15 Vishu						
16 Chitrabhánu						
17 'Swabhánu						
18 Tárana						
19 Pārthiva						
20 Vyaya						
21 Sarvajit	4148	969	1047	4208	1029	1107
22 Sarvadhári						
23 Viródhi						
24 Vicriti						
25 Khara						
26 Nandana						
27 Vijaya						
28 Jaya						
29 Manmatha						
30 Durmukhi						
31 Hévilambi	4158	979	1057	4218	1039	1117
32 Vilambi						
33 Vicári						
34 S'árvari						
35 Plava						
36 S'ubhacrit						
37 S'óbhacrit						
38 Króḍhi						
39 Vis'vávas						
40 Parábhava						
41 Plavanga	4168	989	1067	4228	1049	1127
42 Kílaca						
43 Saumya						
44 Sádháraná						
45 Viródhicrit						
46 Parídhávi						
47 Pramádícha						
48 A'nanda						
49 Ráxasa						
50 Nala						
51 Pingala	4178	999	1077	4238	1059	1137
52 Kálayucti						
53 Siddhárthi						
54 Raudri						
55 Durmati						
56 Dundubhi						
57 Rudhiródgári						
58 Ractáxi						
59 Kródhana						
60 Xaya						

K.	71 S.S.	A.D.	K.	72 S.S.	A.D.	K.	73 S.S.	A.D.	K.	74 S.S.	A.D.
4248	1069	1147	4308	1129	1207	4368	1189	1267	4428	1249	1327
4258	1079	1157	4318	1139	1217	4378	1199	1277	4438	1259	1337
4268	1089	1167	4328	1149	1227	4388	1209	1287	4448	1269	1347
4278	1099	1177	4338	1159	1237	4398	1219	1297	4458	1279	1357
4288	1109	1187	4348	1169	1247	4408	1229	1307	4468	1289	1367
4298	1119	1197	4358	1179	1257	4418	1239	1317	4478	1299	1377

Cycle of Brihaspati.	Cycle 75 K.	S.S.	A.D.	76 K.	S.S.	A.D.
1 Prabhava	4488	1309	1387	4548	1369	1447
2 Vibhava						
3 S'ucla						
4 Pramódúta						
5 Prajótpatti						
6 A'ngi'rasa						
7 Srímukha						
8 Bhāva						
9 Yuva						
10 Dhátu						
11 I's'wara	4498	1319	1397	4558	1379	1457
12 Bahudhānya						
13 Pramádi						
14 Vicrama						
15 Vishu						
16 Chitrabhánu						
17 Swabhánu						
18 Tárana						
19 Pārthiva						
20 Vyaya						
21 Sarvajit	4508	1329	1407	4568	1389	1467
22 Sarvadhāri						
23 Viródhi						
24 Vicriti						
25 Khara						
26 Nandana						
27 Vijaya						
28 Jaya						
29 Manmatha						
30 Durmukhi						
31 Hévilambi	4518	1339	1417	4578	1399	1477
32 Vilambi						
33 Vicári						
34 S'ārvari						
35 Plava						
36 S'ubhacrit						
37 S'óbhacrit						
38 Króddhi						
39 Vis'vávas						
40 Parábhava						
41 Plavanga	4528	1349	1427	4588	1409	1487
42 Kíḷaca						
43 Saumya						
44 Sádháraná						
45 Viródhicrit						
46 Parídhávi						
47 Pramādícha						
48 A'nanda						
49 Rāxasa						
50 Nala						
51 Pingala	4538	1359	1437	4598	1419	1497
52 Kālayucti						
53 Siddhārthi						
54 Raudri						
55 Durmati						
56 Dundubhi						
57 Rudhiródgāri						
58 Ractāxi						
59 Kródhana						
60 Xaya						

K.	77 S.S.	A.D.	K.	78 S.S.	A.D.	K.	79 S.S.	A.D.	K.	80 S.S.	A.D.
4608	1429	1507	4668	1489	1567	4728	1549	1627	4788	1609	1687
4618	1439	1517	4678	1499	1577	4738	1559	1637	4798	1619	1697
4628	1449	1527	4688	1509	1587	4748	1569	1647	4808	1629	1707
4638	1459	1537	4698	1519	1597	4758	1579	1657	4818	1639	1717
4648	1469	1547	4708	1529	1607	4768	1589	1667	4828	1649	1727
4658	1479	1557	4718	1539	1617	4778	1599	1677	4838	1659	1737

Cycle of Brihaspati.	Cycle 81 K.	S.S.	A.D.	82 K.	S.S.	A.D.
1 Prabhava	4848	1669	1747	4908	1729	1807
2 Vibhava						
3 S'ucla						
4 Pramódúta						
5 Prajótpatti						
6 A'ngi'rasa						
7 Srímukha						
8 Bhāva						
9 Yuva						
10 Dhátu						
11 I's'wara	4858	1679	1757	4918	1739	1817
12 Bahudhánya						
13 Pramádi						
14 Vicrama						
15 Vishu						
16 Chitrabhánu						
17 Swabhánu						
18 Tárana						
19 Pārthiva						
20 Vyaya						
21 Sarvajit	4868	1689	1767	4928	1749	1827
22 Sarvadhári						
23 Viródhi						
24 Vicriti						
25 Khara						
26 Nandana						
27 Vijaya						
28 Jaya						
29 Manmatha						
30 Durmukhi						
31 Hévilambi	4878	1699	1777	4938	1759	1837
32 Vilambi						
33 Vicári						
34 S'árvari						
35 Plava						
36 S'ubhacrit						
37 S'óbhacrit						
38 Kródhi						
39 Vis'vávas						
40 Parábhava						
41 Plavanga	4888	1709	1787	4948	1769	1847
42 Kílaca						
43 Saumya						
44 Sádháraná						
45 Viródhicrit						
46 Parídhāvi						
47 Pramádícha						
48 A'nanda						
49 Ráxasa						
50 Nala						
51 Pingala	4898	1719	1797	4958	1779	1857
52 Kálayucti						
53 Siddhárthi						
54 Raudri &c. &c.						

ON ENIGMATICAL NUMERALS.

Some Sanscrit numerals are expressed in words: a cipher is *the sky*. One is *the earth*; Two is *a wing*; Three is *fire*. The four words "Ritu, nāga, vārdhi, *himamsu* (seasons, elephants, sea, and moon) denote SS. 1486. The unit is first named and the thousand is last: in reversed order. Sara, bāhu, Rāma, vasudha, (5, 2, 3, 1,) denote SS. 1325.

Mr. Prinsep's Essay on this subject is printed in the first pages of the Journal (Jan. 1834) of the Asiatic Society of Bengal. This ingenious method is very ancient. I shall here give Mr. Prinsep's list of names with some additions: particularly Jyautisha astrological phrases, which in this list are marked Jy.

These Jyautish phrases are stated in a book called Daivajna Bhushanam.

Every phrase used admits of synonymes: thus for Sea, we may use Ocean, &c.

0. The cypher is expressed by kha, ananta, ācāsam, vyōma: meaning *space*, *sky*, *heaven*.
1. Prithvi, bhū, ku, &c. (the *earth*.) Chandra, Indu, &c. &c. (the *moon*.) Tanu &c. (*body*. Jy.) Also *Rupa*, that is, Form, Face.
2. Paxa, &c. a *wing*. Netra, &c. *eye*; Bahu &c. *arm*. Karna, &c. *ears*. (Kutumbam a *family*, Jy.)
3. Fire: (vanhi, agni, &c.) this phrase is used because in the *yajna* sacrifice there are three fires. Vaisvānara denoting fires. Netra: the three eyes of Siva. Synonymes, Trilochana, Trinetra, and Rama. There are three heroes of this name (Synonymes Dāsarathi, &c.) Guna (qualities; good, middling and bad: called Satwa, rajas, tamoguna.) Jagat: worlds: heaven, earth and hell. (Sahodara, a brother, Jy.)
4. Vedas. (There are four—) Jala-nithi, Ocean. The four seas. Yuga: the four ages: or else *Krita*, the golden age, being first of the four. Koshthu: the corners of a square.—Bandhu (Jy.) a kinsman.
5. Arrows (the five senses as being Cupid's darts.) Gems. (Ratna, &c.) Breaths (prāna,) Sons (Jy.) Suta, putra, &c.
6. Limbs: (anga,) Tastes (rasa,) Tunes (rāga,) Seasons (Ritu,) The Sciences (Tarca, &c.) Foes (Ari *i. e.* the senses or passions: temptations.)
7. Sages: (Muni, Rishi, &c., or Atri who is the first of them.) Musical notes, ut, re, mi, &c. (Swara.) Chhandas (a Veda phrase,) Mountains, (nāga, &c.) Horses (because the Sun drives seven.) Seas (Samudra,) Principles, (dhātu, &c.) Wives (Jy.) as Kalatram &c.
8. Vasu: (a certain class of demigods.) Elephants (the eight that sustain the skies.) Fortune (Jy. mangala, bhuti, &c.)
9. Orifices, or Ways (randhra, as nostrils, ears, eyes, &c.) Planets (graha; including the sun and moon.) Numerals (anca: as 1, &c.)
10. Sides (Dik, Disha, &c. Eight points of the compass with the zenith and nadir.) Avatāra (the ten descents.) In Jy. the phrase Karma is also used.
11. Siva, or Rudra. (In Jyo. Lābha.)
12. Surya: (the sun: one is reckoned to each month.) The Jyo. phrase is Vyaya.
13. Worlds (Viswa.) Cupid: this god being ruler of the 13th day of the fortnight.
14. Worlds (seven above and seven below:) being regions of heaven and hell. Indras, Manus, (the 7 sages twice reckoned.)
15. Tithi, Paxa (Lunations in a fortnight.) Aha (a day, from the same idea.)
16. Kala, a digit. Ashti (a certain measure of verse containing 16 syllables.) A king. (16 being named.)

Mr. Prinsep's list subjoins the following: but they do not appear to be in use: except "Manu" 14 and "Danta" 32.

17. Aty ashti, a certain measure of verse.
18. Dhriti, a certain measure.
19. Atidhriti; (a certain measure.)
20. Nakha, the nails.
21. Swarga, the heavens.
22. Jāti, the tribes.
24. Jina: the Jaina deities.
25. Tatwa: certain beings.
26. Utkriti: (a certain metre.)

27. Naxatra: the constellations.
32. Danta, &c. the human teeth.
33. Deva: the gods.
49. Tána: the tunes.

I have borrowed many of the above statements from Mr. Prinsep.

That the first twelve of these are perpetually used is proved by the following instances. The numerals express dates according to the Salivahana æra.

SS.
235. Pancha, tricam, lochana: that is, Five, three, and eyes.
591. Vastu, graha, bān'a.
980. Vyōm'ebha, randhra: *i. e.* Sky, elephants and ways.
1012. Ravi, vyoma, indu. Twelve suns, a cypher, and the moon.
1029. Nithi, netra, kh'endu.
1043. Jagad, udadhi, viyat, chandra.
1056. Rasa, bāna, kh'endu.—Likewise thus; Rutu, Bāna, vyoma, sasi.
1057. Muni, sara, viyat, indu.
1061. Sasi, rasa, viyat, sōma.
1064. Vārdhi, tarca, ambara, sasi.
1087. Rishi, nāga, kh'endu.
1119. Randhra, subhrāmsu, rūpa, naxatra nāyacah.
1120. Ambara, ravi, sasi.
1181. Chandra, kari, Sasāncau (the *dual* form.)
1209. Nav'āmbara, dwi, himāmsu, that is, Nine, sky, two, moon. Herein numerals are mingled with phrases.
1212. Ravi, cara. Sasi. That is, (twelve) suns, (two) hands, (one) moon.
1225. Bān' āxi-yugmam, sasi: that is, five arrows, two pair (eyes,) moon. In the As. Soc. Journal IV. 124 this is erroneously rendered 1245.
1243. Gun'a, ve'da. Surya: that is, three, four, and twelve.
1266. Suta, tarca, bhánu.
1283. Guna, hasti, netra, vasudha.
1284. Sindhu, nāga, ambaca, sasi.
1301. Sasi, kha, sikhi, chandra.
1317. Saila, chandra, jwalana, Sasi.
1325. Sara, bāhu, rāma, vasudha. Or thus; Sara, bhuja, rāma, chandra.
1326. Ritu, netra, lōca, sasi.
1330. Gagan, āgni, pura, himāmsu.
1373. Indu, gun'a, dhatu, vanhi. In this instance the unit figure is last named: contrary to the general method.
1387. Adri, vasu, agni, sasi.
1449. Nava, vārdhi, veda, sasānca.
1486. Ritu, nāga, vārdhi, himagu.
1493. Rāma, graha, payōnidhi, indu.
1518. Vasu, xmā, bān'a, sītāms'u.
1523. Vaisvānara, lōchana, sara, sudhācara.
1536. Rasa, rāma, bān'a, sasi.
1540. Vyōm' ābdhi, bān'a, chandra.
1544. Véda, samudra, bān'a, chandra.
1595. Bān'a, ratna, indriya, indu.
1619. Randhra, indu, rasa, chandra.
1638. Vasu, rama, rītu, bhū.
1639. Nidhi, agni, mata, sītāms'u.

Notice regarding the names used in the Indian Zodiac. BY C. P. BROWN, ESQ. *(Originally printed in the Madras Journal of Literature, Vol. XIV. for* 1847.*)*

An Essay by Mr. C. M. Whish on the origin and antiquity of the Hindu Zodiac was printed in the year 1827; and has been noticed on a recent occasion in the Royal Asiatic Society. In the Journal of the Asiatic Society of Bengal a paper has now appeared (in No. 167, p. 109) by Mr. J. Muir of the Civil Service, verifying Mr. Whish's assertions. This matter being mentioned to me by Mr. Walter Elliot, I replied that I was already aware of the existence of the Greek words in Sanscrit treatises, having met with them in a manuscript key to astrology. The stanza preserving the twelve names is well known among those Bramins who are skilled in *jotish* (correctly, Jyautisham) which, as Professor Wilson observes, includes "Mathematical, Astronomical, and Astrological Science." Manuscript books on this art are common: there are many in the College Library: which now contains the volumes lately transmitted from the India House: as well as my own collection.

The treatises on (jotish) astrology are all in Sanscrit: and usually open with an explanation of technical words. I shall first notice a large volume called the Jātaca Pārijātam, or Rose of Astrology, (Vol. No. 2330 in the Catalogue.) It is written in the Malayalam character.

It begins with a short hymn addressed to the *Trimurti;* then to the sun, the moon, the planets, and genii. Then follow the twelve signs of the Zodiac, by the well known Sanscrit names.

Mesham, *i. e.* Ram.	Tula, the Scales.
Vrishabham, *i. e.* Bull.	Vrischicam, Scorpion.
Mithunam, *i. e.* Twins.	Dhanas, the "Bow."
Karcatacam, Crab.	Macaram, Sea goat.
Simham, Lion.	Cumbhah, Vessel.
Kanya, Virgin.	Minah, Fishes.

"But, (says the author) the following names are given to these signs."

(Here follows the stanza quoted by Mr. Whish:) it is in the Arya Metre, resembling that used by Horace,

Miserarum est neque amori, &c.

The words are thus spelt: according to Wilkin's system.

Kriya tauru jutuma kulīra.
Lēya Parthōna Jūka, kōrp ākhyāh.
Tauxica, Akōkērō.
Hridrōg Aschsthasih cramaşah.

The same stanza appears in the Vrihajjātacam (written in the Grandham character, MS. N°. 2026) page 6. It runs thus:

Kriya tāvuru jituma kulīra.
Lēya Pārthōna jnāka kōrpy ākhyah.
Tauxica Akōkēro.
Hridrōg asch-āntyabham chētthum.

A third manuscript, in the Telugu character, (vol. 558,) of the Vrihat jātacam, by Bhattotpāla, in page 6 exhibits the stanza thus:

Kriya tāvuru jitumō kulīra
Lēya, Pārdhōna, jūka kaurp'ākhyāh
Tauxica ākōkērō
Hridrōgasch'āntyabham chēd dham.

On comparing the various readings of these three manuscripts, with those printed by Mr. Whish and Mr. Muir, and with the Greek names, the following is the result.

Krios, (the Ram) is written in all Kriya.

Taurus, the Bull: Tāvuru, Tāburi, Tauru.

Didymus, the Twins; Juthuma, Jituma, Jutuma jittuma.

Karkinos the crab; is in all kulīra: the plain Sanscrit word for the crab.

This word *kulira* though uniformly written in all the manuscripts, seems an error for *karkina:* it is the only Sanscrit name used in this verse instead of a Greek name: the metre (Arya vrittam) *can* use *karkina* (a dactyl) in the third seat; and *cannot* use the (amphibrach) kulira in irregular seats: viz., 1st, 3d, 5th, 7th. See Colebrooke's Essay on Sanscrit Poetry, Vol. 2, page 72 note. Captain Jervis in his Volume on Weights and Measures, Bombay 1836, p. 132, has pointed out these Greek words in the Sanscrit canons. He seems to have read *kurku*, which is more like the Greek word. I believe karkina to be the proper word.

Leon, the lion, is uniform in all, Lēya.

Parthenos the virgin; parthōna, Pārthēya, and Pardhōna.

Zygus, the scales; jūka in four MS. and jnāka in a fifth.

Scorpios, kōrpya, korp, koppyār.

Toxicos, the archer, is uniformly Taukshica: —which may also be written Tauxicah.

Aigokeros, the sea goat, is uniformly written ākōkērō.

Hydrochoos, Aquarius, is written Hridrōga, in all but Mr. Whish's copy.

Ichthyes, the fishes. Isthusi, Aschsthaisih. These words resemble the dative, ichthusi. In three manuscripts this word is abandoned: being hard to express in Sanscrit characters.

The three manuscripts I have consulted are ancient: the first quoted is perhaps two hundred years old: it is one of those received last year from the Honorable Company's Library in London. The other two are perhaps half as old: they belonged to my own collection. All three are written on palm leaves. The verses are familiarly known to most of the Bramins who have had occasion to study astrology.

Mr. Whish also cites a Sanscrit verse which mentions the Sun, Mercury, Mars, Jupiter, Saturn, and Venus (called in Greek Helius, Hermes, Ares, Zeus, Kronos and Aphrodite) by the names Heli, Hema, Arah, Jyōk, Kōnah, and Asphujit. In the Brihajjatacam I have read this verse: which deviates only in one name, reading (in 558) Jyos for Zeus. This is a yet more apt coincidence.

GENEALOGICAL NOTICES.

Some of the Hindu Rajas trace their progenitors for five, others for ten or fifteen centuries. To this they usually add a fictitious genealogy, extending the lineage into fabulous ages; and commence with the earliest Sanscrit heroes of the Kali Yugam: who are named Parixit and Janaméjaya: thus the old English historians derive the British kings from the Trojans. One of the lists is laborious and precise enough. It runs thus, commencing with the Kali Æra, 3101 years Before Christ.

Before Christ Years.	Kali Years.	First Year of King named	Length of Reign.
3101	1	Parixit, - - -	64 years.
3037	65	Janaméjaya, -	143
2894	208	Raja Narendra MR., -	140
2754	348	Sāranga Dhara, -	214
2540	562	Sūdraca MR. - -	154
2386	716	Vicramarca, - -	1745

Thus far the names are fabulous. The prodigious reign of Vicramarca embraces a period of which nothing is known.

641	2461	Bhoja MR., - -	144
497	2605	Nandana Chacravarti,	62
435	2667	Tribhuvana Chacr. -	57

From this date the "Chola" names are Tamil.

378	2724	Uttunga Chola, -	32
346	2756	Kulō ttunga Chola, -	15
331	2771	Rajendra Chola, -	9
322	2780	Tiru mudi conda Chola,	18
304	2798	Kariccāla Chola,	21
286	2819	Arindava, - - -	13
270	2832	Warayūr, - -	17
253	2849	Sengaliní, - - -	15
238	2864	Mannalanda, - -	12
226	2876	Manu nī ti kanda, -	15
211	2891	Vāk-kanda, - -	14
197	2906	Ala poranda, - -	8
187	2913	Tirun'ōtti, - -	15
174	2928	Arilōn kanda kondan,	62
112	2990	Jayan-conda, - -	12
100	3002	Krimicanta, - -	20
80	3022	Tondaman, - -	12
68	3034	Bhūtaccanda, - -	45
23	3079	Sengu-oranda, -	14

Before Christ Years.	Kali Years.	First Year of King named	Length of Reign.
9 Until A.D. 1.	3093	Sōlāna Chola,	11

The next names are dated in years that follow (A.D. 1.) the Christian Æra.

2	3104	Kangonda Chola, -	11
13	3115	Sundara Pándya Chola,	40
53	3155	Bōdhappa Chola, -	24

Here the list terminates, before A.D. 79; when the Salivahana reckoning commences. This list, though merely conjectural, exemplifies the Hindu method. I have translated it from an original which uses only Titles as dates, and is worded thus:

"In the first year of the Kali yugam lived king Parixit who ruled until the year Chitrabhanu: 63 years; and Janamejaya ruled 143 years from the year Swabhanu until Visvavas: and Raja Narendra ruled 140 years from Parabhava until Krodhana &c. &c.

In the Chronological tables printed in the foregoing pages, the names are mentioned merely in order of time. It may be convenient to subjoin a few Genealogical tables: which I copy out of various manuscripts collected by Colonel Mackenzie. Wishing to convey authentic statements, I transcribe these lists from the Telugu or Canarese originals, unaltered; as regards the later or historical period: the mythological names which begin many of the lists appear needless.

The first list is one noticed in the preface to Colonel Wilks's History of Mysore: it is entitled "The succession of the Kings of Mysore, from ancient times." Colonel Wilks translated from a Persian version: but the manuscript I use is the ancient Canarese original from which the Persian statement was framed. This Canarese document fills two volumes (No. 1926 and 1721) in the Mackenzie library. They are written with white chalk upon (kaditam) pages made of cloth covered with black plaister. Transcripts have been prepared on English paper at my desire.

GENEALOGY OF THE RAJAHS OF MYSORE.

(In this list W denotes Wadeyar, and A denotes Arasu; that is, King.)

A.D. SS.

Appanna Timma R. His sons were A'rvélla Chām A. Wadeyar, and Dāsappa W. and DRW. The sons of DRW were Chōla Chām A. W. and Krishna W.

1327 1249 The son of Chola Chām AW. named Pedda Chāma RW. was crowned.

1396 1318 And Krishna W's son was named Betta W. the second son was RW.

Pedda Chāma W's eldest son was Chama RW.

The 2d son was Bettada Chām R.

3d son was Madrica DRW.

4th son was Chenna RW.

1399 1321 The next was Narasa RW; he
1401 1323 was the son of RW: and the second son was Nanja RW; and the 3d was Bettad'aiia:
1432 1354 the 4th was Immadi RW.

1435 1357 Kanthīrava Narasa RW.

1447 1369 Elayūru DRW.

Mari DRW.

1478 1400 Dodda RW.

Chikka Devaiia.

1486 1408 Next came the son of Immadi RW. named Chama RW.

1492 1414 Chinna DRW. whose son was Kanthīrava Narasa RW. The second was Pedda Krishna RW. born in SS. 1444.

1614 1536 Immadi Krishna RW; whose younger brother was Nanja RW.

1647 1569 Nanja RW. son of Immadi.

1712 1634 Chāma RW.

1799 1721 Krishna RW.

The dates here mentioned are apparently those of the coronations; I have omitted the specifications of the number of years, months and days each raja reigned. The dates are given very minutely as regards lunar days, and names of years: but all the numerals of years are omitted; and I have supplied these in the margin. There are long genealogical details which also I have omitted: stating merely the names of the reigning rajahs.

THE YA'DAVA RA'JAS.

The following list is copied from a record written in the Tamil language: in a folio volume (marked No. 819,) in the Mackenzie Library

The earlier part of this list is perhaps veracious as regards the names: but the dates seem fictitious. The 19th Raja Pratapá Rudra is known to have ruled Warangal, or Orangolu (now called Wantimitta near Cuddapa) in A.D. 1319—1335 and in this list his reign is dated SS. 1013—1070; that is, A.D. 1091—1148.

The original document specifies the Titles of the first and last year of each prince. But it will suffice to give the numeral of the first year in each reign. And to this I have added the dates A.D. In this list Y. R. will denote "Yādava Rāja."

AD.	SS.	
77	1	The Chera, Chola, and Pandya Rajas.
157	79	
806	729	
808	730	Sri Ranga Yādava Rāja.
833	755	Vīra Nārāyana Y. R.
856	778	O'mana Y. R.

A.D.	SS.	
877	799	Tiru Vēncata Y. R.
899	821	Verankanni Y. R.
913	836	Gand'a Gōpāla Y. R.
938	859	Narasinga Y.
950	872	Kambali Y.
965	887	Bukkanna Y.
987	909	Vīra Narasinga Y. R.
999	921	Immadi Narasinga Y. R.
1007	929	O'yā Y. R.
1019	941	Pāl'iya Y. R.
1028	950	Vasudēva Y. R.
1040	962	Tiruvādi Y. R.
1055	977	Kaṭiki Y. R.
1069	991	Bhujanga Y. R.
1081	1003	Sālava Nārāyana Y. R. This was the latest Yadava: being conquered by
1091	1013	PRATA'PA RUDRA D. of Warangal. But this reign is here dated 220 years too early. The same list proceeds thus: the numerals shewing the year in which each reign begins.
1149	1071	Ballāla Raya.
1236	1158	Ana Vēma Reddi. In truth he lived at least a century later.
1313	1235	Bukka Raya ruled Vijaya nagar.
1327	1249	Hari Hara Raya.
1341	1263	Vijaya Bukka Rāyalu.
1354	1276	Gajaki DR
1362	1284	Dēva Rāya. (This is certainly one century before the true date.)
1369	1291	Virūpāxa Rāya.
1374	1296	Mallic A'rjuna R.
1381	1303	Rāma Chandra R.
1390	1312	Sāluva Kaṭhāri R.
1397	1319	Deva RMR
1412	1334	Gaṇḍa YMR.
1417	1339	Kumāra Kamba Y. R.
1428	1350	Sāluva Kaṭanka DR.
1477	1399	Immadi Kamma R. (Perhaps meant for Immadi Kathari Narasinga R. who lived in A. D. 1503.)
1488	1410	Vīra Narasingaiia R.
1509	1431	Krishna DMR. (this date is correct.)
1529	1451	Achyuta DR.
1542	1464	Sadā Siva R.
1564	1486	Tirumala D. R.
1572	1494	Sri Ranga D. R. who ruled until [A.D. 1585] SS. 1507.

Here the list terminates. I preserve it because it very possibly gives a correct list of names: but its Chronology will not bear investigation, in the earlier centuries: regarding the latest rajas however, it seems to be correct enough. The original manuscript, written in the Tamil character, contains some errors in Titles, which it may be useful to notice because they occur in many documents.

1 Prabhava is misspelt thus 40 "Parabhava"
30 Durmukhi.................55 "Durmati"
41 Plavanga.............35 "Plava"
13 Pramādī....................47 "Pramādīcha"
54 Raudri is misspelt thus..57 "Rudirodgari."

The numerals here appended to each name are never used: just as we use no numerals regarding months. Just as the name alone shews us whether the 3d or the 5th month of the English year is meant: so the name alone shews the place of a year in the Hindu list of sixty years.

THE VIJAYA'NAGAR DYNASTY.

The town ruled by Hari Hara Raya and his successors was called (perhaps at various times) by nine names: 1. A'pé or Hampeh. 2. Nāgar-caṭṭu. 3. A'négondi. 4. Pampā-xētram. 5. Vidyānagaram. 6. Jayapuram. 7. Pānḍava-vijayāpuram. 8. Vijaya-nagaram. 9. Rāya-paṭṇam.

The following genealogy, originally printed by Mr. Campbell, professes to be copied from the "Gutpurtee manuscript" in Colonel Mackenzie's collection. No such document exists in that Library: nor does the name appear in Professor Wilson's descriptive catalogue thereof. The genealogy, wherever found, appears veracious: but it has often been printed incorrectly.

A.D.	SS.	
1336	1258	Hari Hara Raya (The First) was crowned at A'négondi.
1350	1272	He was succeeded by his brother Bukka Rāyalu.
1379	1301	Hari Hara Rayalu the Second.
1401	1323	Vijaya Bukka Rayalu.

A.D.	SS.	
1418	1340	Palla Bukka Rāyalu.
1434	1356	Gaṇḍa Deva Rayalu.
1454	1376	Rāja Sēkhara Rāyalu.
1455	1377	Vijayalu.
1456	1378	Prauḍha DR; also called Pratāpa DR.
1477	1399	Vīra R.
1481	1403	Mallic A'rjuna R.
1487	1409	Rāma Chandra R.
1488	1410	Virūp-āxa R.
1490	1412	Narasimha R.
1495	1417	Narasa R.
1504	1426	(A regency.)
1509	1430	Krishna Rayalu; the second son of Narasa Rayalu by a concubine.
1530	1452	Achyuta DR. (son of Narasa Nayac, who was the son of Iswara Nayac.)
1542	1464	Sāluva Timma Razu, who was the minister: during the minority of Aliya Rama Razu son of Vīra Narasimha Rayalu: whose period is included: *Aliya* (in Canarese) means son-in-law: he having wedded the daughter of Krishna Rayalu.
1564	1486	Sadā Siva Raya, who was the minister, took the government.
1569	1492	Period of Revolutions.
1572	1494	Tirumala Rayalu the younger brother of Aliya Ram Raz, held the rule for a few days; and then was succeeded by his son Sri Ranga R. who was followed by his brother, named,
1585	1507	Vencata pati R. who was followed by his brother, named,
1630	1552	Rama R. also called Rama DR.

Then from SS. 1560 until 1574 (A.D. 1638 until 1652) there were wars with the Musulmans.

THE CHALUKYA GENEALOGY.

The antiquity of the Chāluk-ya race has been proved by Inscriptions dated in the fifth century of the Christian Æra: and these are published by Mr. Wathen in the fifth volume of the Journal of the Royal Asiatic Society. Professor Wilson (Descr. Cat. '. cxv.) has pointed out that there were two Chalukya dynasties: the elder reigned at Kalyān in Karnāta: the other in Kalinga.

The Chāluk-yas were of the Jaina religion originally: but the latest rajas of this name became converts to the Vishnu creed. The history regarding this may be seen in Buchanan [Hamilton's] Mysore, vol. 2, page 80. It is there stated that a celebrated reformer of the Vishnu religion named Rāmānujāchāri was born in SS. 932 (A.D. 1010.) That Yādava-puri (now called Tonnūr) was the chief city of a prince named Ballāla Raya: and he was converted from the Jaina to the Vaishnava creed, (about SS. 1060) by Rāmānujāchāri: who changed the prince's name to Vishnu Vardhana Raya.

The same author (Buchanan-Hamilton) gives some other particulars regarding Vishnu Vardhana: who, as here seen, was of Jaina descent. The Telugu translation of the Maha Bharata is dedicated to this raja: whose ancestors are there unnamed: because their names would have betrayed their heretical genealogy. To conceal the names of his forefathers, a fable has been invented; which asserts that his birth was supernatural.

About a century before the birth of Vishnu Vardhana, the Chaluk-ya rajas thought fit to have an æra of their own, beginning in SS. 938 that is, A.D. 1016. The Chalukya calculation appears to have lasted less than a century and a half: and Vishnu Vardhana lived within the first century of that æra: not of the Salivahana æra.

Colonel Mackenzie's account may be seen in the Introduction to Campbell's Teloogoo Grammar: it is there stated that the family was subverted in the second century of the "Christian Æra." It should be, in the second century of *their own æra*: of which the first year answers to A.D. 1016.

Another raja named Kubja Vishnu Vardhana, son of Inda Rāz, is mentioned: whose grandson bore the same name. But nothing has been proved regarding the date of his reign. He perhaps was some minor baron.

One VISHNU Vardhana has been said (See the same Grammar, page x.) to be of the SAIVA creed: it would be just as credible were he said to be of the MAHOMEDAN creed.

Three others so named are mentioned as having lived in earlier ages. But regarding them or their creed nothing is known, and no proof exists that the Vishnu creed wás introduced at an earlier period. In those ages the Canarese and Telugu nations worshipped either Siva, or Jina ; or (more generally) petty village gods : such as Poturaz, Gangamma, Poleramma, or other local saints: resembling the Yagathamma (St. Agatha) and Maryamma (Mary) now worshipped in Madras.

That their raja should bear the name of Vishnu is unlikely: the creed of that god having been introduced, by Ramanujachari, at a later period.

The following are the only Chalukya Rajas whose reigns, in the Telugu country, are recorded on marbles. These rulers generally used an æra of their own: which was numbered in a method not clearly understood: however, the usual Cyclic Titles are used, and these have sufficed to furnish a clue: though the numerals 1, 2, 3, &c. are used separately for each reign.

A.D.	SS.	Title.	
1016	938	Nala	This was the first Chalukya year.
1068	990	Kilaca	Chaluk-ya Bhūlōca Malla.
1111	1033	Khara	Beṭṭada Raya, who was afterwards called VISHNU VARDHANA.
1139	1061	Siddharthi	Jagad Eca Malla.
1150	1072	Pramōduta	Trailōkya Malla Deva.
1156	1078	Dhatu	Tribhuvana Malla, also styled Bizzana Devara, alias, Nija Bhuja Bala Chacravarti, alias, Jagad-Eca Vīra Bizzala Dēva.
1168	1090	Sarvadhāri	Kālachurya-Chacravarti-Rāya-Murāri-Sōyi-Deva.
1176	1098	Durmukhi	Kalachurya-Chacravarti, alias, Nissanca Malla, alias, Sancama Deva, alias, Yādava Nārāyan'a A'hava Malla Deva.
1184	1106	Krodhi	Chalukya-Chacravarti-Sōmēswara Deva-(alias) Tribhuvaua-Malla Deva.

After this date the name Chalukya rarely occurs: and seems to be used without a proper claim. It will be observed that these dates and names do not everywhere correspond with those found in the Koncan genealogy. The Chalukya dynasty thus terminated and was succeeded by the Yādavas: whose genealogy has already been given.

The marbles that record the names of the Cha-luk-ya rajas always specify the name of the year, but usually omit the Salivahana numeral: substituting the Chaluk-ya numeral: which is reckoned on some plan hitherto unexplained and apparently irregular. For instance SS. 1088, 1094 and 1097 are all, in various records, styled "the 31st year of Tribhuvana Malla the Chalukya." The year Parābhava is in one place called the 40th; elsewhere the 51st Chalukya year.

The first of the Chalukya rajas is named Tribhuvana-malla; likewise Trailokya Malla: likewise Jagad-ēca-malla: likewise Bhuvanaica-malla: all four names merely denote imperial sway: while Tailapa seems to have been his personal name.

The same titles, omitting personal names, were continued to his son and grandson: hence arose the error of supposing him to have ruled for ninety years. Some lists state that the first raja was Jagad-ēca Malla: the next was Bhuvanaica Malla; the third was Tribhuvana Malla: and the next rulers were the Ganapatis.

As the poet and grammarian Nannaia Bhatta, who wrote the A'di Parvam in Telugu, lived in the reign of Vishnu Vardhana, we are now in possession of the æra when that author flourished: and at that period the Telugu language had already attained classical perfection.

The Mahabharat was commenced by the grammarian named above: but was continued by Erra Pragada, and completed by Ticcana Somayāji: who likewise translated into Telugu metre a great part of the Ramayan. He died in the year SS. 1120 that is, A.D. 1198. This date is recorded in verse, thus

క॥ అంబర రవి శశి శాకా
బ్దంబులు జన, కాళయుక్తి, ఆశ్వయుజమాసం
బంబర- మణి-, ప్రభా- ని
భంబగు తిక్కయజ్వ బ్రహ్మము పొందెన్.

"Ambara, ravi, sasi, s'ācā
B'dambulu zana, Kālayucti, A's'wija māsam
B'ambara-man'i-prabhā-ni
Bhamb'agu, Tikka Yajva, Bramhamu ponden.

"The venerable poet Ticca obtained heaven the month A'swija, in the year Kalayucti which has the numerals denoted by Sky (0.) Suns (12.) and Moon (1.) [That is by reversing the figures, SS. 1120.]

In the Descriptive Catalogue (vol. 1. 267) Professor Wilson has recorded this verse: but that distinguished scholar was on this occasion misled by an *erroneous* copy; which gives the date, incorrectly, SS. 1210; (A.D. 1288) and this is not the year named Kalayucti, but Sarvadhari.

In a former publication (Essay on Telugu Literature, printed in the tenth volume of the Madras Journal of Literature, 1839,) I also was deceived, regarding the date of Krishna Rayalu, an eminent raja of Vijayanagar. I quoted a Telugu epigram which learned bramins usually cite; they believe that it fixes his decease in the year "Tarana 1387" that is A.D. 1464. But later research has convinced me that the person named in that verse is not the celebrated patron of Telugu literature, who lived until the year Virodhi, SS. 1451 (A.D. 1529.) In fact we know nothing regarding the personage mentioned in the epigram.

I have already shewn that some genealogical tables framed by bramins are delusive: another instance may be given. Some of these lists are so adjusted as to place the celebrated Krishna Rayalu's death in the year "Tarana 1387" sixty five years too early.

ON SOME FRAGMENTS OF EARLIER HISTORY.

Few inscriptions have been discovered relating the Hindu History of the Peninsula earlier than A.D. 1000. And of these few some are wrongly dated: thus becoming doubtful. For instance: the year SS. 90 (A.D. 168) is correctly 42 Kilaca (the forty second Cyclic Title:) whereas it is quoted by the name (29.) Manmatha: which name appertains to SS. 76, not 90. A deviation of two or three years in the numeral is common enough: but a deviation of more than five years will generally stamp a document as false. Again; we find one name Vīra Ballala Deva, placed in "SS. 100 Sarvari the 34th Cyclic year; whereas in truth SS. 100 is Siddharti, the 53d Cyclic Title. And Madhava Raya is stated to have ruled Vidyānagar in "SS. 104 Paridhavi." But this title appertains to SS. 93, not 104.

The earliest trust-worthy date is that of a celebrated patron of literature named Bhoja Raja: whose reign is placed between SS. 118 and 194 (A.D. 196—272.)

Under the year SS. 378 (A.D. 456) some legends place Cherumān Perumallu, who is stated to have become a follower of Mahomed. This is referred to in several books: it is obscurely alluded to in Briggs's Ferishta vol. 4, p. 532. But were the date correct, this person must have lived before the birth of the prophet whose creed he embraced.

In SS. 390 (A.D. 468) Madhava Varma appears to have abdicated, after a reign of one hundred and thirty years in favour of his son Padma Sena.

In SS. 411 (A.D. 489) reigned Pulakesi Satyāsraya: See Journal of Royal Asiatic Society vol. 5, p. 344.

The following dates occur regarding (Y. R.) the Yadava Rajas.

A. D.	SS.	Title.	Raja's Name.
808	730	Sarvadhari	Sri Ranga Yādava R.
857	778	Dhatu	O'man Y. R.
877	799	Hevilambi	Tiruvengada Y. R.
743	821	Siddharti	Peranganni Y. R.
758	836	Bhava	Ganda Gopala Y. R.
781	859	Hevilambi	Nārāyana Y. R.
794	872	Sadharana	Kampali Y. R. and also Bhuvan Eca Malla.
956	878		Immadi Vallevatu.
965	887	Krodhana	Buccanna Y. R.
987	909	Sarvajit	Vira Narasimha Y. R.
999	921	Vicarī	ImmadiNarasimha Y.R.

All we know, true or false, of these rajas is, the date of their reigns: and their having bestowed certain lands on certain priests. For the Inscriptions on stone are generally intended for this one purpose. The rights so conferred were long ago abolished by the Musulman invaders.

THE KONKAN GENEALOGY.

The princes of Vijayanagar descended from a long line of forefathers; a list of whom I have already printed. I will now again give that catalogue as recorded in an ancient Tamil volume called Konka-Desa-Rajaccal; or, Konkana Raja Vamsāvali.

The original document has already appeared in the Madras Journal of Literature, Volume XIV. The book is little more than a record of various gifts presented by the successive rajas, to gods and bramins. Each gift is minutely described and dated, with precision.

The earliest names herein given are as usual fabulous. The list commences a little before the beginning of the Christian Æra. Numerals are attached to each raja's name.

1. Vīra Rāja Chacravarti was the first ruler of the Konkan country: he was of the Farmer tribe; called Vellāla, or Reddi.

2. Govind Raja.

3. Krishna Rāyalu.

4. Kāla Vallabha Rayalu.

5. Govinda Rāyalu: who lived in Swabhanu, (the 17th year of the Cycle) which is (SS. 4) the fourth year of the Salivahana æra: answering to A.D. 83.

6. Chatur-bhuja-Kannera Deva Chacr. who likewise was of the farmer tribe.

7. Trivicrama D. Chac. This was the first raja who quitted the Jaina creed and became a worshipper of Siva. He conquered the Chola, Pandya, Kerala, and Malayala countries. He lived in SS. 100 [A.D. 178.] "in the year 53 Siddharti."

It will be observed that in this list the years are generally quoted both by their titles, and also by the numeral representing their place in the Cyclic list of sixty names.

8. S. Konkani Vara Dharma Mohadi Rayalu. His reign is dated SS. 111 year Pramoduta. [A.D. 190.]

9. Mādhava Mahādhi R.

10. Hari Varma Mahādhi R. SS. 210. [that is AD. 289.]

11. Vishnu Gōpa MR. He founded Dalvana-puram: which was afterwards called Talac-cāḍu. He abdicated in favour of his adopted son named,

12. Mādhava Mahādhi Raya, who ruled until the said raja Vishnu Gopa had a son born to him named,

13. Krishna Varma. He was succeeded by Mādhava Raya's son named,

14. Ḍinḍīcara R. The next raja was Krishna Raya's younger sister's son, and named,

15. Koukaṇi Mahādhi R.

Then the country passed into the hands of Chandra Ḍinḍiga R. In the year Prabhava SS. 288 (A.D. 367.)

16. His son named Dhruva Nīti R. succeeded him, and ruled the countries of Kērala, Pānḍya, Chōla, Dravida, A'ndhra, and Kalinga; "and obtained the epithet *Dhruva Nīti* or Absolute Justice." His son was

17. Mushkara Pāndya: who was styled Bramh-āri Rāya, or Foe of Brahmins. His son was

18. Tri-vicrama Rāya: who was succeeded by

19. Thū Vicrama Rāya. He lived in SS. 461 (A.D. 539). He bore the title GAJAPATI or Lord of Elephants. His son was

20. Konkani MR.

21. Raja Govinḍa R. He was partial to the Linga-dhāri sect.*

He ruled at Mucunda-paṭṭanam.

22. Siva Kāma Raya was a devout worshipper of the gods. The date of his reign is preserved in the words "Vastu 1, graha 9, bana 5. That is, SS. 591 Pramōdūtā=A.D. 670.

23. Prithvi Konkana Mah-ādhi Raya who ruled until Parthiva SS. 608=A.D. 685.

24. Raja Malla DR.

25. Garḍa DMR.

26. Satya Vākya R.

27. Guṇad Uttama R.

28. Raja Malla DR. who reigned from year Vicari, SS. 800 (A.D. 879.) until SS. 816 Ananda (A.D. 894.)

"And then followed the CHOLA RA'JAS, who ruled the Koncan. The first was

29. Vijayadā Raya. His son A'ditya Varma ruled Tanjaur in the Chola country. He ruled the Konkan and his capital was Talaccadu [afterwards called Seringapatam on the Kāvēri.]

*Yet we know from other documents that Basawa the founder of this sect was not heard of before A.D. 1160.)

His son was

30. Vīra Chōla R. also called Vīra Chola Nārāyana Razu.

31. Tējōditya R.

32. Parāntaca R. also called Arimāli: he ruled at Tanjaur. His wife was Chitri and with his corpse she was burnt. He had many sons; one was

33. Divya R. who conquered Madura. He took the title Ariditt.

34. Ari Vāri Devara, raja of Tanjaur, ruled the Chola and Dravida countries: His brother conquered Madhura; but restored it to its original lord, the Pandya. Ari vara Devara conquered the countries of Kerala (Malayalam) Collūr, Indragiri, Nilagiri-durgam and other places: but the Kerala raja's general named Bhīma Rao repelled the invasion and slew the son of the king who thereupon marched northwards through the Kalinga country as far as the river Narmada (Nerbudda.) He also completed the pagoda at Chidambaram (Chellumbrum) which had been partly built by his father and grandfather. His capital was Kerayūru in the Talaccadu [Seringapatam] country; and he named it Rāja Rāja Puram. He lived in the year Visvāvas, SS. 927 [A.D. 1005.]

Here commences the HOISALA Dynasty, descended from the Yādavas.

This list as usual commences with Bramha and certain heroes: but omits the immediate predecessors of VOISALA, elsewhere called, Hoisālā: originally called *Sālăh*, but changed into Oyi-sāla.

35. Vina-yāditya ruled Talaccadu [Seringapatam] and seized some villages in the Tulava country. Year Sādhārana SS. 991 [A.D. 1070.] He was succeeded by his son Vallālen, that is,

36. Ballāla Raya: he was of the Jaina creed. Year Axaya " SS. 1015." [But the true number would be SS. 1008.] His son was,

37. Betteda Rāya, who took the title BETTEDA VISHNU VARDHANA. He was king of Talaccādu (Seringapatam) and also part of the Tulava and Concan countries: also Malayala and Codugū [Koorg.] also in the north Jātīmālā, and (eastwards) A'lambādi. He long waged war with the raja of Kerala [Malayālam]. The wife of Vishnu V--dhana was Sāntala Dēvi, who was at first of the Jain creed; but embraced the Vishnu religion. For in the year Vicrama SS. 1021 [otherwise 1023, A.D. 1100] the saint Rāmānuja-chari [the celebrated reformer of the Vishnu sect] persuaded the raja to embrace the Vishnu creed. This raja died in the year Ananda, SS. 1055. [A.D. 1134.]

Here the chronicle specifies various gifts of land, bestowed by this rajā on Jains and Brahmins: with the dates.

38. Raja Narasinga Raya became raja of Talaccādu, and dwelt at Dora-samudram. He bestowed many lands on bramins. He died in the year Vijaya SS. 1094 (AD. 1173). His son was

39. Ballala Raya, whose mantri (minister) was Chandra Mauli. His dalavayi or general was Ke's'iv' E's'wara.

40. Sōmēs'wara came to the throne in SS. 1155 (A.D. 1233) and was crowned in his father's life time.

41. His son was Vīra Narasinga Raya who was crowned at Talaccadu in SS. 1205 [A.D. 2283.] His *mantri* was Perumān Danda Nayaca and his *sēnapati* (general) was Prama- chamūpati.*

Continuation.

GENEALOGY OF THE YA'DAVAS.

The earliest progenitor was Yādava Sangama Raya† [spelt in the Tamil original S'ankama.] He had five sons, named Bukka Raya, and Hari Hara R. and Sambara R. and Mārāpah R. and Muttapa R. Of these the eldest, named

* The names of ministers and generals merit notice: because these occur in many Inscriptions, wherein these personages style themselves princes.

† Regarding him there is an Inscription in Sanscrit verse. It was sent by Colonel Mackenzie to the venerable Colebrooke and is published in his Essay on Ancient Monuments (Essays, London 1837, vol. 2, page 254—266.)

In this it is stated that in the Yadu race there arose a king named SANGAMA, who had [five] sons named Harihara, Kampa, Buccaraya, Ma'rapa, and Mudgapa. The victories gained by Bucca-raya are described in the usual inflated style. He ruled Vidya'nagar. His queen Gaura'mbica, bore a son named Harihara, in whose reign this Inscription was written. It is dated SS. 1317 Dhatu: that is, A.D. 1395.

Bukka Raya came to the throne : he had a son, named,

42. Hari Hara Raya : who is also called Hari Hara Bukka Rayalu, king of Vijayanagar.

43. His son was Deva Rayalu, SS. 1270, Virodhi [A.D. 1379,] whose son was

44. Vira Hari Hara Raya. He fought and conquered the (Pārsī) Persians [that is, the Musulman invaders.] Then he marched (with his general Gunḍa Danḍa Nātha) into many countries as far as (Sindhava) Scinde. He was succeeded by

45. Vishnu Deva Maha Raya ; who is merely said to have built certain pagodas, and endowed them with lands for sacred purposes.

46. He had two sons named Mallic Arjuna and Immadi D. R. His army was commanded by Timmanna Nayac, in the year Yuva SS. 1377, [A.D. 1455]. They were succeeded by Vira Narasinga Rayalu, [who appears to have usurped the throne.]

DYNASTY OF VIRA NARASINGA RAYALU.

His descent is described, beginning as usual with the fabulous ages. From the Lunar* race descended the Yādavas: from whom sprung the Tulavas. In this family arose Timma Raz, king of Vijaya-nagar. His son was,

47. Vīra Narasinga Raya who ruled Vidyānagar. § His *mantri* was Ud-danda, and he conquered Vijaya Raz the ruler of Kērala (Malayalam). He made a treaty with the Pa'nḍya rājah of Madhura. He vanquished the Kalinga and Bengala countries.† He slew the Gajapati [that is, the ruler of Orissa] and vanquished many Mahomedans. Then he took the title Lord and Master of all kings and princes.‡ He died in SS. 1401, year Sarvari [A.D. 1480.] He had two wives, [literally, women : one being a concubine] named Tippaxi and Nāgala Devi : to them were born two sons named Vīra Narasinga Rayalu and KRISHNA RAYALU. Another wife [lit. woman] named Woyambica bore him two sons named Ranga-Rayalu and Ach-yuta Rayalu.*

48. In year Sarwari, SS. 1401 [A.D. 1479] Vīra Narasinga Rayalu was crowned : he lived until year Rudirodgari SS. 1425 [A.D. 1503.]

49. He was succeeded by his younger brother KRISHNA RAYALU :† who was crowned in the year Ractacshi, SS. 1426. [1504.] His younger brothers were Achyuta Raya and Ranga Raya. This raja built the forts at Vijayanagar, and Penucota and Chandragiri and other places. He marched into the Dravida (Tamil) country wherein he conquered the towns of Kānchī (Conjevaram) Senji (Gingee) and Veloor. This raja's elder brother Vīra Narasinga Rayu [the preceding ruler] had attacked the raja of Um-mat-toor near Sivasamudram, but had failed. It was defended by Chicca Rayalu : and Krishna Rayalu conquered this town after a siege of one year. Thence he marched to Sri-rangapatnam [Seringapatam] which town he fortified and made it his capital in the year Prabhava SS. 1434 [Error for 1429 which is Prabhava, A.D. 1507.] He conquered the Codugu, Kerala, Malayalam, Chola, and Panḍya countries. Then he marched northwards and made friendship with the raja of KALINGA, and the rulers of the HINDU DESAM.‡ He also subdued Ghurjara, (Guzerat) and Magadha. He conquered many Turacas (Musulmans) and then returned to Vijayanagar where he died in SS. 1462|| [A.D. 1540.]

* The Solar and Lunar races (Sarya Vamsam and Chandra Vamsam) like the Pelasgi and Hellenes of the Greeks, are often mentioned : every raja pretending to trace his lineage up to one of these aboriginal stocks. See Raper's Survey of the Ganges, in Asiatic Researches Vol. XI. quarto, p. 523.

† Throughout the present document the chronicler when writing a list of conquests sets down all the names of countries he can think of. Here we find a Cannadi raja spoken of as conquering Bengal : but in truth he was about to be vanquished by the Musulmans.

‡ This title, implying universal dominion, is a mere flourish, added to the names of several rajas. Many English writers have been deceived by such idle phrases, which are just as fabulous as the "King of France" which so many of our English monarchs used to assume.

* A clearer account is given in another page of the present volume.

† See Madras Literary Society's Journal, No. 32, page 40.

‡ In the Inscription already noticed as translated by COLEBROOKE, in the twelfth verse is a similar mention of one HINDU RAYA : whom that learned translator supposes to be the Hindu'pati of Bundelkhand. A conquest of that country by Krishna Raya would not be a whit more marvellous than others averred in these documents : which make him ruler of every country known to the lying chronicler.

|| Erroneously here written SS. 1400. But, even if we did not know the true date from other sources, we are here told that his s[illegible]ccessor reigned for eighteen years : which settles the date.

50. He was succeeded by his younger brother Ach-yuta Rāyalu: who laid out more money than his predecessors on gods and bramins.* He died in the year Siddharti, [SS. 1480 A.D. 1559] after a reign of eighteen years.

51. He was succeeded by Krishna Rayalu's son Rāma Raya, [who is elswhere styled Aliya Rama Raya.] His younger brother was [Aliya] Timma Raya. Their army was commanded by Sadā Siva Raya†, who fought the Musulmans but at last he was beaten and driven first to A'ne'gondi which he lost: but then the raja made peace with the invaders and retained Penagonda. He had three sons named Sri Ranga Raya, Rama Raya, and Vencatapati Raya. After ruling for fifteen years he died in SS. 1494 [A.D. 1572.]

52. He was succeeded by his eldest son Sri Ranga Raya in the year Yuva. (SS. 1497.) He placed Seringapatam under the command of his brother Rāma Raya; who soon died. His younger brother Vencatapati Raya commanded Chandragiri.

53. This raja [Sri Ranga Raya] was succeeded by his son Tirumala Raya, who was crowned in the year Parthiva, SS. 1506 [A.D. 1585.] In SS. 1512 year Khara [A.D. 1591] his grandfather Sri Ranga Raya died at Penagonda, and was succeeded by his son Vencatapati Raya.

Then Seringapatam was besieged by Vīrappa Nayac of Madura; who was defeated and driven back to his home. But Matteh Vencatapati, commander of the Seringapatam army, betrayed his master and left him (Tirumal Nayudu) a prisoner at Madura: while he usurped the throne. Tirumal Nayudu escaped, and made his way home: he took up his abode at the village of Mālinga Kesari, where the rebels attacked him. But he was rescued by Raja Wodayar king of Mysore, who marched to Seringapatam and in the year Saumya SS. 1531 (A.D. 1609) he conquered that city and made it his capital.

Here the history terminates. In making this English abstract I have omitted more than three quarters of the volume: consisting of minute and tedious details, regarding grants of land, made by the Rajas to bramins; and long since abolished by the Musulman conquerors.

* Pity that neither gods nor bramins saved him from the Musulman conquerors!

† In many inscriptions Sada Siva is described as a king: but he was in fact only the general.

ON THE KALI ÆRA.

The Kali Æra or Age of the World commences in the Year 3101 Before Christ: and the Hindus have measured the years after that date by dividing time into Cycles of sixty years each. The learned state that the 68th Cycle commences in SS. 889, (A.D. 769) which is A: Kali 4068. And the 83d Cycle begins with SS. 1789. AK. 4968 which answers to A.D. 1867. Such is the statement made by Native Astronomers: yet they further declare that the Kali Yuga is reckoned from Friday (Suddha) the first day of the moon, in the month Chaitra in the year Pramádi; which is not the first but the 13th year of the preceding Cycle. For the First Cycle is reckoned from Prabhava which is the 48th year of the Kali Æra.

This date is recorded in Francis Buchanan (Hamilton's) Mysore, vol. 3, p. 110. In this work the dates are oddly printed. A.D. 1335-6 for instance, is expressed A.D. $133\frac{5}{6}$. The same author wrote a work on "Eastern India" which Mr. Montgomery Martin has published in three thick volumes, in which he gives himself out as the author: and in the third volume there appears the first hint that he is merely the publisher.

ON THE HEJRI, FASLI, VILAYATI AND SAMVAT.

The Musulman Æra named Hejri was introduced into the Indian Peninsula about A.D. 1600; and the Fasli reckoning cannot be discovered in any document earlier than A.D. 1650.

The Hejri system, which I have printed according to Warren's Tables, was clearly intelligible: but out of this arose the Fasli, or "harvest" which very probably was intended to suit the Hindu method. The year A.D. 1800 was Hejri 1215, but the Fasly year was 1209, being six years less. In 1850 it is seven years less.

The Hejri year, of 360 days is used only by Musulmans: who use no other method.

The Fasli is used solely by Hindu clerks in the East India Company's service. During the Musulman government the Fasly was loosely used; thus the year Krodhi (A.D. 1784) is Fasli 1193, but in some documents is 1194. The year Saumya (A.D. 1789) is numbered Fasly 1198; but in some places this becomes 1196, and elsewhere 1199.

About the year A.D. 1800 when the country became subject to the English, the Fasli year happened to commence on the 13th of July. Whereupon the English constituted that day as the beginning of the Fasly year: which thereupon was metamorphosed into a solar reckoning: but devoid of months: being a mere official year. The Hindus at the present day (only the clerks in Government employ) quote the Fasly by the last two figures alone. Thus A.D. 1820 is called "Fasly Twenty-nine" AF. 1229) which it is the fashion to mention in Hindustani numerals: thus "Untis Fasly" means 1229. And Fasly 1239 (A.D. 1830) is called Untalis Fasly: that is, 1239.

Thus in Munro's Report (26th July 1807 Fifth Report p. 785) he speaks of the Survey rent in 1215 (meaning Fasly 1215, that is, A.D. 1806;) and 1217, 1218, meaning A.D. 1808 and 1809.

Among the Inscriptions and other documents collected by Mackenzie there are a few which state the Hejri date in Arabic numerical words. Thus (written in Canarese characters) sittu, sabaain alaf=6+70+1000 that is, AH. 1076.

It appears that the "Vilayati" (Willaeti) and Sambat (Samvatsara) used in Bengal are nearly the same as the Fasli. Thus the First Regulation of A.D. 1793 is dated the "1st of May; answering to 21st of Bysaak (Vaisakha) 1200, Bengal æra; 21st Bysaak 1200 Willaity; 6th Bysaak 1200 Fusly: 6th Bysaak 1850 Sumbut; and 19th Ramzan 1207 Hegeree [5th Rep. p. 738.]

ON THE COLLAM ÆRA.

The town of Collam, which we call Quilon has given its name to the æra used in the Malayalam country. That æra is reckoned from about A.D. 825. Accordingly A.D. 1850 is the year 1025-6 of this reckoning.

The English Almanac printed at Travancore gives the following list of thirty-two Sovereigns of that country: with the specified date A.D. of their accession.

1 Mārtanda Varma Raja came to the throne in A.D. 1335
2 Eravi Varma, ...1375
3 Kulasekhara 1382
4 Chara Wadeya Martanda Varma Kulasekhara Perumalu Raja 1383
5 Vainati Muttu Raja 1444
6 Mārtānda Varma Raja 1458
7 A'ditya Varma Raja 1471
8 Eravi Varma 1478
9 Mārtānda Varma 1503
10 Eravi Varma 1504
11 Martanda Varma 1528
12 Udaya Martanda Varma 1537
13 Karula Varma 1560
14 A'ditya Varma 1563
15 Udaya Martanda Varma 1567
16 Eravi Varma Kulasekhara Perumallu 1594
17 Vira Varma 1604
18 Eravi Varma 1606
19 Unni Karula Varma 1619
20 Eravi Varma 1625
21 Unni Karula Varma 1631
22 Aditya Varma 1661
23 Ummay Ammal Rāni (Queen) 1677
24 Eravi Varma 1684
25 Unni Karula Varma 1718
26 Rama Varma Raja 1724
27 Vanji Mārtānda Varma Kulasekhara Perumallu 1729
28 Vanji Bala Rama 1758
29 Bala Rama Varma 1798
30 Gauri Laxmi Bāi (a Queen)....A.D...1811
31 Gauri Pārvatī Bāī (Queen) 1815
32 Vanji Bala Rama Varma Kulasekhara Perumallu Raja 1829
33 The present Raja 1847

In this as in some other genealogies, the same name appears again and again as applied to various rajas.

ON LITERARY FRAUDS.

Some papers printed in the Proceedings of the Royal Asiatic Society by Mr. C. M. Whish, (who died in the year 1833) evince his skill in Mathematical investigation and in Sanscrit scholarship. The article *Viga Ganita* in the Penny Cyclopædia, and pages 325, 326 of the same volume, having mentioned Mr. Whish's discoveries, with a surmise that they may be forgeries, I offer the following description of their origin.

I have reason to believe that Mr. Whish himself was the author. This belief is founded on information given me by Visvambhara Sastri, one of the tutors in the Madras College.

This learned bramin had been intimately acquainted with Mr. Whish and assured me in the year 1840 that the Sanscrit stanzas conveying mathematical rules were constructed under Mr. Whish's guidance in A. D 1820 by Ayya Sastri, a professor of Sanscrit law, who after being long employed in the College, became a Law Officer in the Court of Sudr Udalut. Ayya Sastri was a free thinker and derided all religions. From time to time, while framing these verses, he shewed them to my informant, who laughs at the credulity of the English in believing them ancient.

That the verses cited by Mr. Whish are apocryphal may easily be shewn. In the third volume of the Transactions, p. 509, we have a rule regarding the proportion that the diameter bears to the circumference of a circle. But this is quoted " from the Tantra Sangraham." Now this name denotes a " Summary of Magic." In the East India House, in the Madras College, and in Mr. Whish's own collection of books at the Royal Asiatic Society's Library, there are many books on the Tantras: but no one of them is named the Tantra Sangraham. Nor does this name occur in the Tantra Rajam, in the commentary on the Sarada Tilacam, or other similar treatises, which are profuse in quotations from Tāntrica authorities.

Doubtless the Tantras often mention Magic numbers, but use these in a manner as devoid of sound reason as the " Babylonic numbers" alluded to by Horace.

Were a modern professor write mathematical rules in Greek verse, and attribute them to " Eupolis Cratinus or Aristophanes," the writers of old Comedy, the fraud would not be more daring.

Another fabrication was described to me by the same person. Before the custom of burning widows alive was abolished, some enquiries were made in Madras regarding passages in Sanscrit law books, which were said to condemn the practice. Ayya Sastri, being required to produce some texts, readily undertook to fabricate a few laws written in Sanscrit verse, prohibiting such murders.

He took care to quote respectable authors in proof: when these passages were forwarded to Calcutta, the forgery was easily detected; but, adds my informant, an English translation was prepared and published at Madras without any mention of the detection.

The Sthala Puranas or Sanscrit legends regarding the sanctity of the idols worshipped at various pagodas, usually pretend to be extracts from the Skanda Puran, a book of vast extent, of which no complete copy has been discovered. See Wilson's learned Preface to his version of the Vishnu Puran, page xlvi. These furnish additional proof of the scorn of veracity so common among the Hindu framers of legends supporting the local superstitions.

I may adduce another forgery. In the Asiatic Journal for July 1819, (vol. viii., p. 28,) there are some Sanscrit lines regarding vaccination describing the process and its effects.

This statement is very properly criticized in the London Christian Observer for July, 1819, page 441. The author says " It's minuteness leads me to feel a suspicion that it is a mere forgery."

A letter written by the Abbé Dubois in the year 1805 (and printed in the Asiatic Annual Register for 1806 at the beginning of the Bengal occurrences) is regarding Vaccination: and is entirely silent regarding such Sanscrit rules, had they existed they must have been known to the bramins whom Dubois consulted. Ayya Sastri was at Madras at the period when this very statement appeared: and in all probability Mr. Whish was the writer of the letter conveying the story.

Another mark of affinity is, that the writer quotes a "Săctya Grandham" attributed to Dhanwantri.—Now Dhanwantri is the Indian

Hippocrates: and a "Sāctya Grandham" "is a treatise on magic and on the worship of Demons." To attribute such a work to a physician is unreasonable.

The genealogies given in the present volume may suffice to elucidate the names of persons mentioned in the Cyclic Chronology. Among the Mackenzie manuscripts some other lists exist, which do not seem to merit publication. Some English essayists have attempted to reconcile the various lists of names. I have thought it better to give them just as they stand in the original documents. This plain statement has betrayed many inconsistencies, and shewn that few records dated earlier than A.D. 1400 can be relied on, unless supported by Inscriptions. Indeed the older portions of these lists are often as fabulous as some which are recorded in the peerages of other nations.

ADDITIONS, AND CORRECTIONS.

A.D. 1138 Read thus. Accession of Jagad ēca Malla at Kalyānam. Vishnu Vardhana ruled Rajahmahendri and is now styled R.R. Narendra.

1199 (Add) Choda Rayalu.

1235 (SS. 1157) SVP. Vicrama DMR. Inscription at Seven Pagodas. See Madras Journal No. XXX. p. 56.

1272 For Dwara, read Dora.

1435 Mummadi Praudha R. came to the throne: he ruled until A.D. 1480.

1566 The Vaddeh barons are the Karnātaca rajas.

1634 Should be a line lower: opposite 8 Bhava: and so of the next four years.

1666 This is SS. 1588, or elsewhere 1581.

1674 This is 1596 or elsewhere 1593.

1695 Chikka Rāja Wadeyar.

1718 SS. 1640 or 1638.

1735 Nadir Shah usurped the crown.

1747 Death of Nadir Shah.

1760 Krishna R. Wadeyar.

The following belong to the Index, &c.

Page.

30 Mummadi Praudha R. 1435—1480.

30 Pratāpa Rudra (Kakati) reigned eighty-eight years.

31 Ticcanna, the poet, died in A.D. 1198. See page 58.

31 Vema Reddi. One person bearing this name was the son of Allāḍa Bhūpāla. A.D. 1434.

32 Waddiyar. (At the end read thus.) The third 1679—1724. Krishna R. W. 1760.

52 (Four lines from the foot,) "No. 167, page 809."

52 SS. 1440 Kha (0) jaladhi (4) manu (14.) This is an instance of "Manu" being used for *fourteen*.

53 Dr. Mill has printed the verse thus, in page 399 of the Journal of the Asiatic Society, July 1835.

Kriya tāburi jituma Kulīra Lēya, pārthēya yūka, &c.

60, 61 Talaccaḍu is a town on the Kāvērī, about fifteen miles south east of the modern town of Seringapatam.

THE END.